Directing Language Skills

Senior Authors:

William F. Hunter
Clinical Psychologist
Minneapolis, Minnesota

Pauline L. LaFollette
Former Teacher
Fort Wayne Community School
Fort Wayne, Indiana

Contributing Author:

Justine Maier
Educational Writer
Clayton, Missouri

Consultants:

Charlotte B. Fosher
Special School District
St. Louis County, Missouri

Carlton H. Green
Special School District
St. Louis County, Missouri

The Learning Skills Series: Language Arts
Acquiring Language Skills
Building Language Skills
Continuing Language Skills
Directing Language Skills

Webster Division, McGraw-Hill Book Company
New York St. Louis San Francisco

Acknowledgments

The authors and editors wish to thank the following people for their valuable contributions in testing the book: Mrs. Sandra Birenbaum and her class, Southview School, St. Louis County Special School District, St. Louis County, Missouri; Mr. Daniel Costello and his class, Hiram Neuwoehner School, St. Louis County Special School District; Mrs. Barbara Leardi and Mrs. Peggy Salden and their classes, Collinsville High School, Collinsville Community District No. 10, Collinsville, Illinois.

Editorial Direction: Neysa Chouteau
Design: Virginia Copeland
Editing and Styling: Mary Lewis Wang
Production: Leo B. Painter

Cover design by Joe Gray.
Cover art developed from photos by
Editorial Photocolor Archives,
Dan O'Neill, Laima Druskis,
Susan McKinney.

Illustrations by John Winkelmolen,
Richard O'Leary; from Publishers Graphics:
David Brown, Ray Burns, Eulala Conner,
Bert Dodson, Pamela Ford.

ISBN 0-07-031334-2

Contents

Name ____________________ Date __________

Chapter 1: FINDING INFORMATION

Capitalization and Punctuation

Telling sentences start with a capital letter and end with a period. Rewrite the sentences below. Start each sentence with a capital letter. End each sentence with a period.

1. last January, Pat Allen turned sixteen

   ____

2. she studied hard and passed her driver's license test

   ____

3. her older brothers were mad

   ____

4. they would not like letting Pat have the car

   ____

5. there would be fights in the Allen family

   ____

Reading Carefully

Read page 1 again. Then answer these questions.

1. Is Pat older or younger than her brothers? ____________

2. Were her brothers glad or mad that Pat got her driver's license?

____

A Learner's Permit

Before Pat got her license, she got a learner's permit. It was called a Temporary Instruction Permit.

3. Fill out the permit below. Tell about yourself. Use capital letters where needed.

TEMPORARY INSTRUCTION PERMIT

Borges   Eva   Belo
Last Name   First   Middle

21 ashland St
Street Address or RFD

Taunton   Mass   02780
City   State   ZIP Code

Height 5' 4"   Weight 122 l

Eyes Brown   Hair Brown

Date of Birth March 12 1946

★ Discussion

Talk about Pat and her brothers. First talk about what happened. Then talk about why there would be fights in the Allen family. Last, talk about a way to end the fights.

Name ______________________ Date ____________

Discussion

Can you name the days of the week? Can you name the twelve months? Can you name ten states? Can you name six cities?

Proper Nouns

Names of days start with a capital letter. Write the names of four days. Start each name with a capital letter.

1. Monday
2. Tuesday
3. Wednesday
4. Friday, Saturday

Names of months start with a capital letter. Write the names of four months. Start each name with a capital letter.

5. April January
6. February March
7. May June July
8. August September

October November December

Names of people start with a capital letter. Write the names of four people you know. Start each name with a capital letter.

9. ____________
10. ____________
11. ____________
12. ____________

Names of cities start with a capital letter. Write the names of four cities. Start each name with a capital letter.

13. New Bedford
14. Boston
15. Providence
16. Los Angelos

Names of states start with a capital letter. Write the names of four states. Start each name with a capital letter.

17. Massachutssetts
18. Mossouri
19. Massachuksets
20. Mossoury

Mosouri

Names that start with a capital letter are called proper names, or proper **nouns**.

Nouns

Naming words are called *nouns.* Some nouns are proper nouns. They start with capital letters. Some nouns are not proper nouns. They do not start with capital letters. They are called common nouns.

The words below are naming words, or nouns. Some are proper nouns. Proper nouns start with capital letters. Put a circle around each noun that should start with a capital letter.

1. day	**2.** yesterday	**3.** thursday
4. wednesday	**5.** tomorrow	**6.** sunday
7. tuesday	**8.** friday	**9.** saturday

Rewrite each word below. Start the proper nouns with a capital letter.

10. june June	**11.** month month
12. august August	**13.** january January
14. year year	**15.** february Febrary
16. october Octoker	**17.** september September

Circle each noun that should start with a capital letter.

18. jane	**19.** man	**20.** ellen
21. boy	**22.** woman	**23.** maria
24. uncle	**25.** chris	**26.** edward

Rewrite each noun below. Start the proper nouns with capital letters.

27. chicago Chicago	**28.** new york New York
29. city city	**30.** dallas Dallas

Name ______________________ Date __________

Alphabetical Order

A B C D E F G H I J K L M N O P Q R S T U V W X Y Z

a b c d e f g h i j k l m n o p q r s t u v w x y z

To put words in alphabetical order, look at each first letter.

application car door engine
license office

If the first letters are the same, look at the second letter.

same school seat show

If the first and second letters are the same, look at the third letter.

than then this those

1. Write these words in alphabetical order.

name capital

letter day

month letter

capital month

day name

2. Write these words in alphabetical order.

drive drive

test passed

tried puzzle

passed test

puzzle tried

3. Write these words in alphabetical order.

pan pan

press phone

pound pound

punch press

phone punch

4. Write these words in alphabetical order.

child champ

chunk chew

champ child

chew christmas

Christmas chunk

The Telephone Directory

When Pat was ready to get her driver's license, she looked in the telephone directory. She looked for "Driver's License."

1. Which page below would show "Driver's License"? Write *A* or *B*. ____

A
402 Drisdale-Drury
Drisdale, A. 216 Elm . . **862-4807**

B
560 Gore-Graves
Gore, H. 372 Oak . . . **754-2617**

2. This is what Pat found for "Driver's License":

DRIVER'S LICENSE—
SEE MISSOURI—STATE OF—
DEPT. OF REVENUE

Which page should Pat turn to next? Write *A* or *B*. ____

A
370 Dennis-Derry

B
1038 Missel-Missouri

★ Finding Information

Check your telephone directory. Does it show "Driver's License"? __________ Look under your state. Find a place you might call about a driver's license. Copy the name. ______________

____

★ Using the Telephone

Pretend to call the driver's license office. Ask when it is open. Say "thank you" before you hang up.

Name ______________________ Date __________

Newspaper Ads

FORD Air, steering, brakes, clean, make offer. 123-4567

NOVA Three years old. Orange, automatic, very good. Must see. $1,695. 765-4321

CHEVY Clean, like new, $695 or best offer. 432-3456

VW Easy on gas, clean, new tires. Five years old. Make offer. 111-2222 after 6:00 P.M.

Read the ads for used cars. Then do the exercises below.

1. The owner of the Chevy is asking $695.

2. The VW has new tires.

3. The Nova is three years old.

4. The owner of the VW should be called after 6:00 P.M.

5. The owners of the Chevy and the VW want you to make an offer.

Writing Sentences

6. Write a sentence to tell which car you like.

I like the Nova.

7. Write a sentence to tell which car you don't like much.

I dont like the VW

Proofreading

Does each sentence make sense? Did you start it with a capital letter? Did you end it with the right mark? Did you capitalize proper nouns?

Capitalization and Punctuation

All sentences start with a capital letter. Telling sentences end with a period. Asking sentences end with a question mark. Here is an asking sentence:

Does this sentence end with a question mark?

Put a question mark at the end of each sentence below. Put a circle around each letter that should be a capital letter.

1. can you read ads for cars in the newspaper yes
2. will the ads talk about trade-ins ___
3. do you know what a trade-in is yes
4. does the newspaper have ads for new cars yes
5. does the newspaper have ads for used cars yes
6. does it cost money to put an ad in the newspaper yes
7. why do people put ads in newspapers ___
8. will there be ads about trade-ins yes
9. do people want special values when they buy cars yes
10. do you know what a special value is yes
11. did you ever see a car that is a special value No

★ Discussion: Word Study

Tell what you think these words mean. Listen to what your classmates say. Try to agree on the best meanings. Write the meanings below.

special value ________________________________

____

trade-in ________________________________

____

Name ______________________________ Date ______________

Capitalization and Punctuation

Some of the sentences below should end with a period. Some should end with a question mark. Put the correct mark at the end of each sentence. Put a circle around every letter that should be a capital letter. Remember: proper nouns need capital letters.

1. people who want to sell cars put ads in the newspaper ___
2. they put their telephone numbers in the ads ___
3. do you know why they do this ___
4. you may see an ad for a '56 chevrolet ___
5. what do you think the '56 chevrolet should cost ___
6. what kind of car should cost $2,000 ___
7. do you think a honda motorcycle should cost $2,000 ___
8. can you think of a new car that costs less than $3,000 ___
9. why is it a good idea for some people to buy a new car ___
10. why is it a good idea for some people to buy a used car ___

Word Study

Write a complete sentence using each word. Remember: a sentence is a group of words that makes sense.

telephone newspaper license

11. ______________________________

____

12. ______________________________

____

13. ______________________________

____

Newspaper Ads

Sell things you no longer need with a CLASSIFIED ADVERTISEMENT	2 lines 2 weekdays	$3.00
	2 lines 6 weekdays	$7.00
	2 lines Sunday and Monday	$4.50

Call 531-5555 *Perry News*

The ad above is for a newspaper section called *classified ads* or *want ads.*

Read the ad carefully. Then answer these questions.

1. What number do you call to place an ad? ______________

2. What is the name of the newspaper? ______________

3. How much does an ad for Sunday and Monday cost? ________

The Telephone Directory

The Yellow Pages of the telephone directory have an index. Here is part of the index:

Automobile Damage Estimators See Appraisers . .21, 22

Automobile Dealers— New Cars 28–32

Automobile Dealers— Used Cars 33, 34

Automobile Driving Instruction See Driving Instruction 136, 137

4. What pages show new car dealers? ______________

5. What pages show used car dealers? ______________

6. Use your telephone directory to find the number of a new car dealer. Write the number here. ______________

Name ______________________________ Date ____________

The Owner's Manual

When you buy a new car, you get an owner's manual. An owner's manual is very helpful. It has directions for many things, such as filling the gas tank and putting air into the tires. It tells how much the car weighs, how much horsepower the motor has, how long and wide the car is. It has drawings that show where things are.

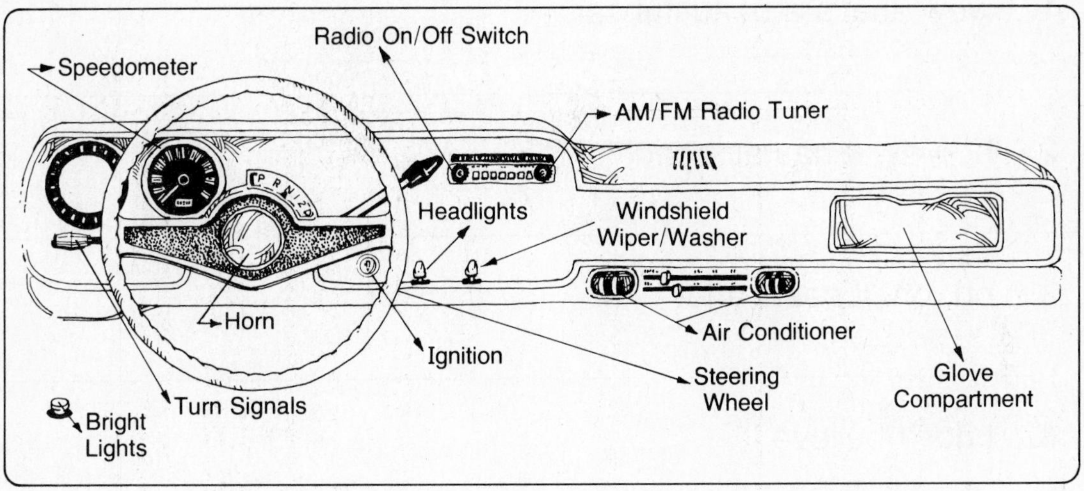

Look at the drawing. Then answer these questions.

1. What word tells where the key goes? ____________

2. What words tell where the left and right turn lights are?

____

3. Does this drawing show a radio? ____________

4. Does the drawing show a tape deck? ____________

5. Does the drawing show an air conditioner? ____________

6. What words name something you use at night on a dark road when no other cars are coming? ____________

7. What words name something you use when it's raining?

____

Exclamation Points

Some sentences show strong feelings, or excitement. These sentences end with an **exclamation point.**

Run for your life!

Rewrite the sentences below. Put an exclamation point at the end of each one. Begin each sentence with a capital letter.

1. wow, that's a beautiful car

____

2. hooray, it has air conditioning

____

3. oh, oh, it costs a lot

____

4. i don't believe it

____

End Punctuation

Add the correct punctuation mark to each sentence.

5. Did you read the owner's manual ___
6. You did read the owner's manual ___
7. Oh, boy, I love new cars ___
8. Hurry! Buy this car right now ___
9. Will you buy this new car ___
10. Where is the owner's manual ___
11. Here is the owner's manual ___
12. Hooray, I found the owner's manual ___

Name ______________________ Date ____________

Pronouns

These words stand for nouns. They are called **pronouns.**

I	me	they	them	he	him
you	it	we	us	she	her

For each noun below, write a pronoun that can stand for that noun. One has been done for you.

1. girl *she* **2.** man ____________

3. house ____________ **4.** dogs ____________

5. boys ____________ **6.** women ____________

7. woman ____________ **8.** car ____________

9. Charles ____________ **10.** Audrey ____________

Fill in the blanks to complete the sentences.

11. I can use two of the pronouns to talk about myself. The two pronouns are __________ and __________.

12. I can use two of the pronouns to talk about myself and other people. These two pronouns are __________ and __________.

13. One pronoun is always written with a capital letter. That pronoun is __________.

14. When I talk about a car, a house, or a tree, I can use the pronoun __________.

★ Finding Information

Find eight ads in the newspaper. Be sure that all of the ads show cars that you would like to buy.

Paste each ad on a sheet of paper. Below each ad, write a sentence that tells you why you like the car.

Pronouns: Naming Self Last

When we speak politely, we always name ourselves last.

She and I would like a ride.

Would you like to ride with **Tom and me?**

Sue and I want to go to the park.

Complete the sentences below. Choose from the words at the end of each sentence.

1. ______________________ would like to take our driving test. (Me and my sister, My sister and I)

2. Have ______________________ come to the right place? (she and I, me and her)

3. Yes, both ______________________ can give tests. (my partner and I, me and my partner)

4. Good! Then can you test ______________________ at the same time? (her and me, I and she)

5. Yes, ______________________ are both free right now. (I and my partner, my partner and I)

Complete each sentence below by naming yourself and another person.

6. ______________________ like to drive.

7. Would you like to drive with ______________________?

8. ______________________ saw the movie.

★ **Speaking Carefully**

After you have completed the sentences above, read each one aloud. Then make up three sentences of your own. Name yourself last in each sentence. Say your sentences aloud.

Name ______________________ Date __________

Newspaper Ads

The classified ads have many sections. Here are some of the sections you might see:

RENTALS	REAL ESTATE
700—Apartments Furnished	805—Farm Land
705—Apartments Unfurnished	815—Homes for Sale
710—Business Places	830—Business Property
730—Houses Unfurnished	

1. You need to rent an apartment. You have no furniture or furnishings. What section advertises the kind of apartment you need? ______________________

2. You own a store. You want to rent it to someone. You could put an ad in section ______________________

3. Where do you look for a farm? ______________________

4. Where do you look if you own your own furniture and want to rent an apartment? ______________________

5. Where do you look if you want to buy a business? ______________________

6. Where do you put an ad if you have a house for sale? ______________________

★ Finding Information

Look in a newspaper. Try to find ads for these things:

A job that you could do
A place that buys coins
A dog for sale
A motorcycle for sale

Recognizing Sentences

It takes more than capital letters and punctuation marks to make a sentence. A sentence makes sense by itself. Here are some words that are not sentences:

A new car with tires.

After the movie and dinner.

Some of the words below make sentences. Some do not. Decide if each group of words is a sentence. If it is, write *yes.* If it is not, write *no.*

1. Tim learned to drive last year. ____________
2. His car a tree. ____________
3. He had to pay $950 to get his car fixed. ____________
4. He $200 nose fixed. ____________
5. Then he had to get a job. ____________
6. What never got fixed? ____________
7. The tree with the nest of birds. ____________
8. Tim got a new car last week. ____________
9. Great big rubber bumpers in front. ____________

Writing Sentences

You should have found four groups of words that are not sentences. Choose three of those. Rewrite them as complete sentences.

10. ____

11. ____

12. ____

Name ______________________ Date __________

Writing Sentences Review

1. Write a question. Use the name of a state in your question.

2. Write a telling sentence. Use the name of a city in your sentence.

3. Write a question. Use the pronoun *I* in your question.

4. Write a telling sentence. Use the name of a day in your sentence.

5. Write a sentence. Use the pronoun *me*.

6. Write a sentence. Use the pronoun *him*.

7. Write a sentence. Use the pronouns *she* and *her*.

8. Write a sentence. Use the pronoun *us*.

Proofreading

Check your work. Does each sentence make sense? Did you start it with a capital letter? Did you end it with the right mark? Did you capitalize the proper nouns?

Word Puzzle

Here are some words. You had some of them in your lessons. Find all of them in the puzzle. Mark them like this:

```
F I N D O
V A I X Z
V U C X O
X W E E O
```

application	special	think
office	quick	driving
alphabetical	that	order
than	rules	glad
used	value	wink
license	thick	

```
O R D R E N S G A L D E S A D O R M
F R O W N I C K T H I R P O R E S A
F V A L E U A L P H A B E T I C A L
I C R O L O V E G L A D C P V O T E
C A P P L I C A T I O N I A I D H C
E O R D E R C S L O T R A N N R I E
S I N K R U L E S U I H L T G E C N
A Q U I C K B O N D E S I O H R K S
Q U I N K E A R U S E D R N C A U E
U S K W I N K R U L E R O C K I T E
```

Riddles

Try to guess the answer to each riddle. If you give up, turn the page upside down for the answer.

1. A horse has four legs. If we call the tail a leg, how many legs will the horse have?
2. What is the longest word in the English language?

1. Four. Calling the tail a leg doesn't make it one.
2. Smiles. There is a mile between the first and last letters.

Name ______________________________ Date ____________

Chapter 2: FOLLOWING DIRECTIONS

Capitalization and Punctuation

The first word of every sentence starts with a capital letter. The name of a person starts with a capital letter.

Rewrite each of the sentences below. Begin each sentence and each proper noun with a capital letter. Add the correct end punctuation.

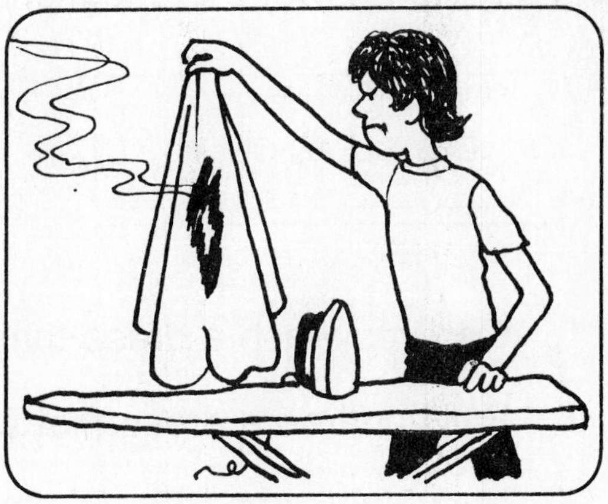

1. fred did not want to iron his shirt

____

2. his sister, jenny, told fred to learn to iron

____

3. do you think jenny should have ironed fred's shirt

____

4. fred did not read the tag in his shirt

____

5. the tag says to use a warm iron

____

6. the shirt burned when fred used a hot iron

____

★ Discussion

Read exercise 3 again. Tell the class what you think. Listen to what others say. See if you agree.

Following Directions

Here are some samples of tags you can find in clothes. Read the tags to answer the questions.

A

DRY CLEAN ONLY

B

HAND WASH SEPARATELY. DRY FLAT. COOL IRON. CAN BE DRY CLEANED.

1. Can you wash a dress that has tag *A*? __________

2. Will you iron a dress that has tag *A*? __________

3. If a shirt has tag *B*, can you machine-wash the shirt? __________

4. Can you put a shirt with tag *B* in the dryer? __________

5. Can a shirt with tag *B* be dry-cleaned? __________

6. If you iron a shirt with tag *B*, what temperature should the iron be? __________

C

MACHINE WASH PERMANENT PRESS. TUMBLE DRY, REMOVE PROMPTLY. DO NOT IRON.

D

HAND OR MACHINE WASH WARM. DO NOT USE BLEACH. TUMBLE OR DRIP DRY LOW TEMP. FOR TOUCH-UP USE COOL IRON. DO NOT DRY CLEAN.

7. If slacks have tag *C*, can you iron them? __________

8. Can you put slacks with tag *C* in the dryer? __________

9. Can you bleach a blouse with tag *D*? __________

10. Can you dry-clean a blouse with tag *D*? __________

11. Can you put a blouse with tag *D* in the dryer? __________

12. Can you iron a blouse with tag *D*? __________

Name ______________________________ Date ______________

Following Directions

Washers, dryers, and irons have dials. The dials show how to set each machine from cool to hot.

1. What temperature is this washer set for? ______________

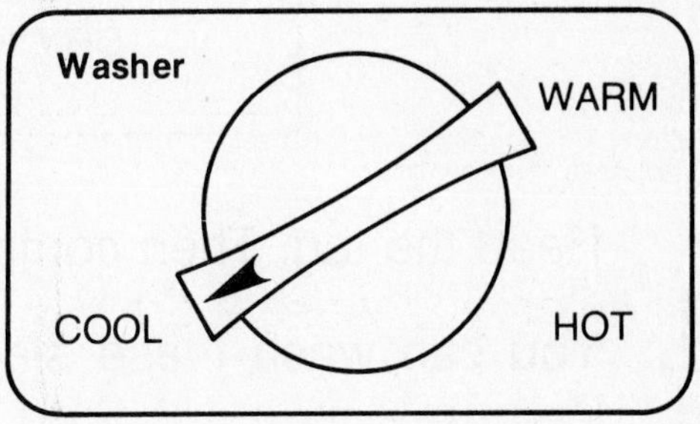

2. What temperature is this dryer set for? ______________

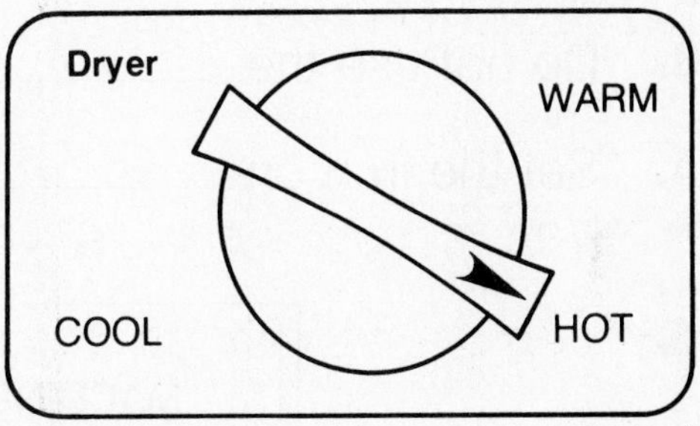

3. What temperature is this iron set for? ______________

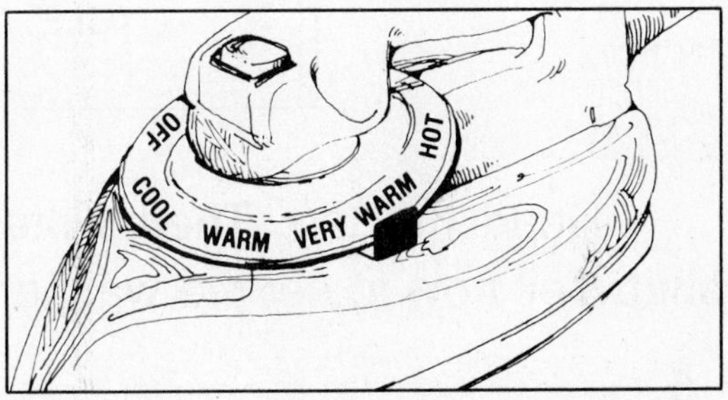

Read the clothing tags. Read the iron dials. Draw an arrow to "set" each iron dial. Make the dial match the tag.

4.

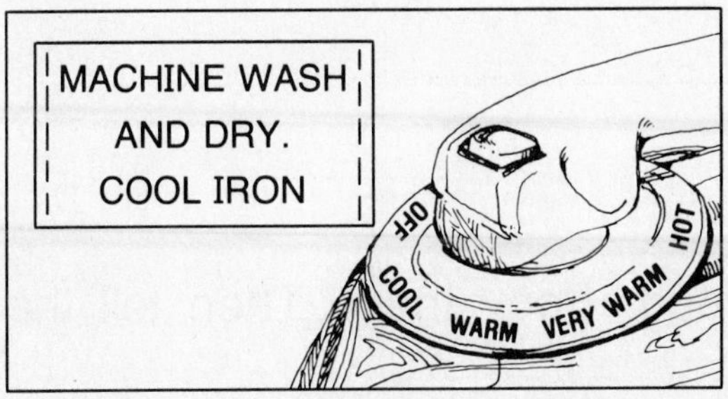

5.

Writing Directions

MACHINE WASH WARM.
NO BLEACH. LINE
DRY. WARM IRON.

Read the tag. Then complete the directions below.

1. You can wash these slacks in the ____________________.
2. You cannot use ____________________ in the wash.
3. Do not use the ____________________ to dry them.
4. Set the iron on ____________________.

MACHINE WASH WARM.
TUMBLE DRY GENTLE
CYCLE. COOL IRON.

Read the tag. Then write directions. Tell how to wash this shirt. Tell how to set the washer, dryer, and iron.

5. ____

____

____

____

____

★ Giving Directions

Find directions on a box of food. Copy them. Then tell the class how to prepare the food.

Name ______________________ Date __________

The Dictionary

dic · tion · ar · y (dik′ shən er′ ē) *n.* A book that explains words.

Look at the dictionary entry above. It is divided into several parts:

dic · tion · ar · y	This part shows the word. The dots separate it into parts, or syllables. This word has four syllables.
n.	This shows the part of speech. It shows that the word is a noun.
dik′ shən er′ ē	This shows how the word is pronounced.
A book that explains words.	This is the definition. It tells what the word means.

Here is another dictionary entry. Use it to follow the directions below.

in · struc · tions (in struk′ shənz) *n.* Directions or orders.

1. Copy the word. ______________________
2. Tell how many syllables in the word. ______________________
3. Copy the pronunciation. ______________________
4. Tell what part of speech the word is. ______________________
5. Copy the definition. ______________________
6. Write a sentence. Use the word in your sentence.

____

____

Word Study

Use words from this list. Complete the sentences below. If you do not know what a word means, look it up in the dictionary.

permanent	bleach	instructions
press	directions	temperature
tumble	machine	iron

1. When you ____________ something, you make it a lighter color.

2. When something will roll or toss about, it will ____________.

3. If something lasts a long time, it is ____________.

4. Sometimes we say that we iron our clothes. Sometimes we say we ____________ them.

5. When something is hot, it has a high ____________.

6. A shirt or blouse that does not have to be ironed has a ____________ ____________.

7. The ____________ on a dryer tell you how to use it.

8. If someone tells you how to do something, she is giving you ____________ or ____________.

9. Two words that mean about the same thing are ____________ and ____________.

10. It is usually metal. It usually has moving parts. It is a ____________.

Name ______________________________ Date ______________

Reading Carefully

Answer the questions below.

MACHINE WASH,
DRY WARM.
USE COOL IRON
FOR TOUCH-UP.

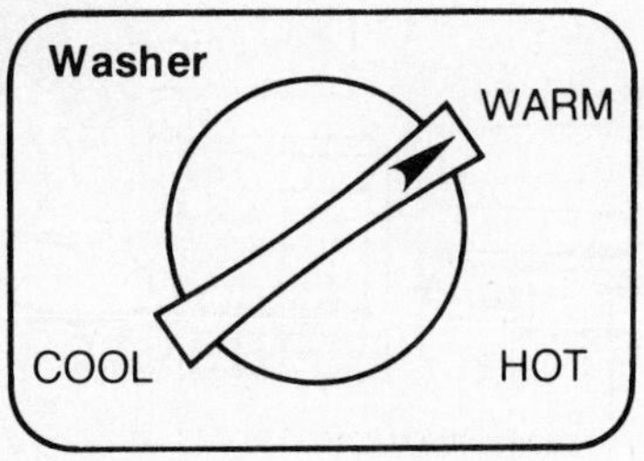

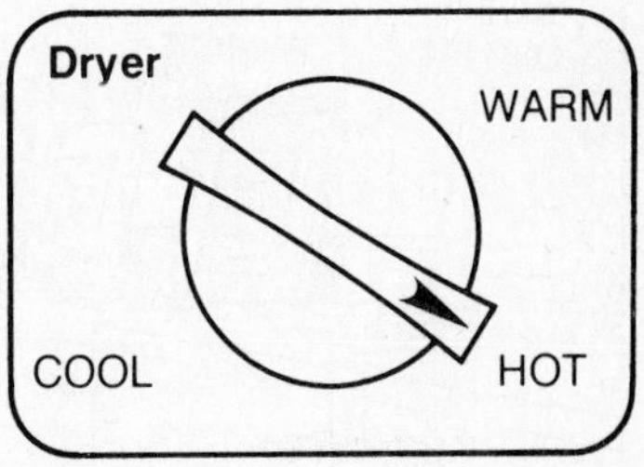

1. Which dial is set wrong? ______________

HAND OR MACHINE
WASH, COOL.
LAY FLAT TO DRY.
DO NOT USE IRON.

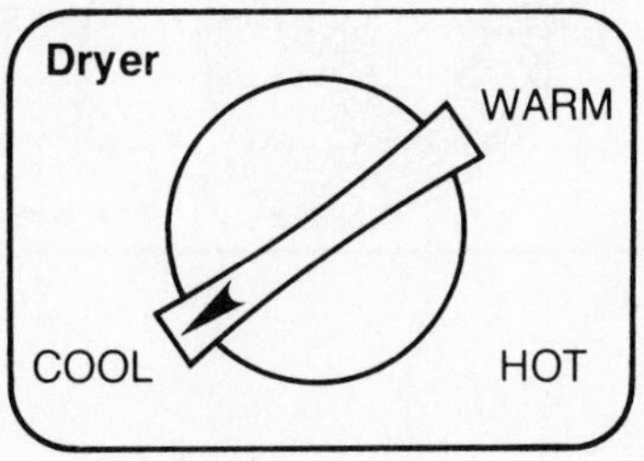

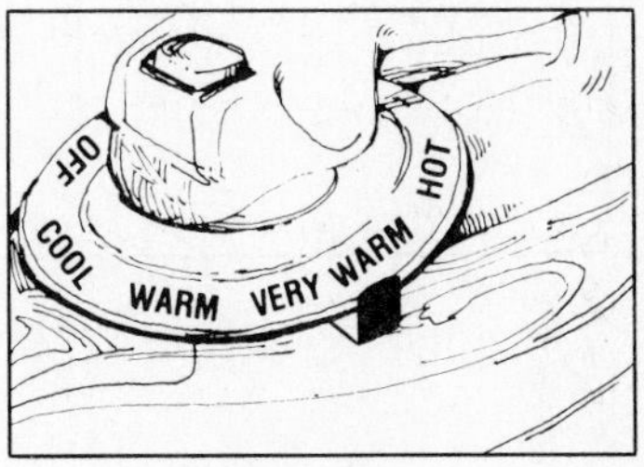

2. Do you need the dryer? ________
3. Do you need the iron? ________

HAND WASH,
LINE DRY.
COOL IRON.

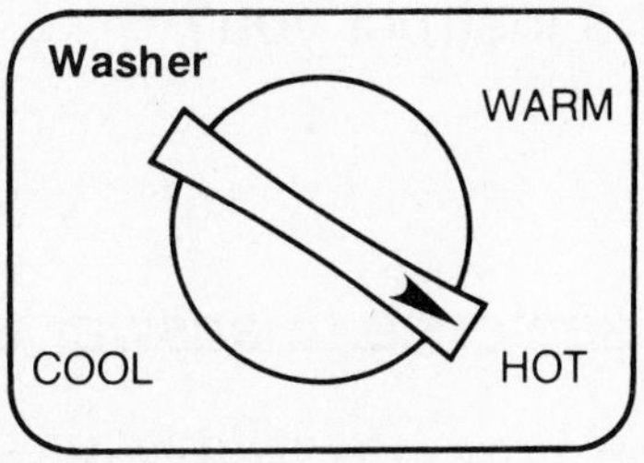

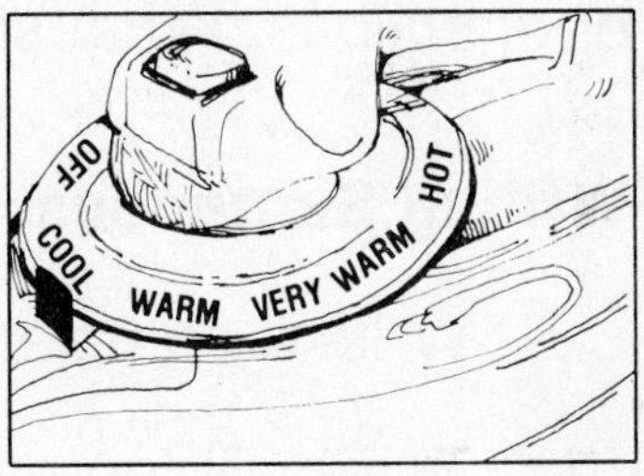

4. Is the iron set correctly? ________
5. Should you use the washer? ________
6. Should you use the dryer? ________

★ Giving Explanations

Choose one of the tags above. Tell the class how you would wash, dry, and iron clothes with that tag.

Discussion

Most Laundromats have signs. Read the signs. Why should people count their socks before they leave? What will too much soap do? What can you buy?

Signs help people to know what to do. They give instructions or directions. What signs instruct you?

Writing Sentences

Write a complete sentence to answer each question.

1. What will too much soap do to the washers?

___

2. Do you think you can buy soap at the Laundromat?

___

Proofreading

Check your work. Does each sentence make sense? Did you begin it with a capital letter? Did you end it with the right punctuation?

Name______________________________ Date __________

End Punctuation

Put the right punctuation mark after each sentence.

1. Laundromats are full of instructions ___
   Are Laundromats full of instructions ___
   Wow, look at the instructions ___
2. Can you buy soap at Laundromats ___
   Hooray, here's some soap ___
   You can buy soap at Laundromats ___
3. Always count your socks before you leave a Laundromat ___
   Whoops, count your socks ___
   Should you count your socks before you leave ___
4. Are directions and instructions the same thing ___
   Directions and instructions are the same thing ___
   I hate directions ___
5. Will too much soap jam the washers ___
   Too much soap will jam the washers ___
   Oh, oh, that's too much soap ___

Writing Sentences

6. Write an asking sentence.

____

____

★ Finding Signs

Visit a Laundromat or a store near your home. Copy three signs that you see.

Finding Sentences

CITY HALL	OUT OF ORDER

Find four complete sentences in the words below. Rewrite each sentence. Start each sentence with a capital letter. End it with the correct punctuation mark.

there are all kinds of signs some of them tell what is for sale other signs tell you where you are why should you be able to read signs

1. ____________________

2. ____________________

3. ____________________

4. ____________________

There are five complete sentences in the words below. Find each sentence. Write it correctly.

Fred works at the Laundromat he is very good at his job the dryers in the Laundromat do not always work Fred has to put a sign on the broken dryers do you know what the sign says

5. ____________________

6. ____________________

7. ____________________

8. ____________________

9. ____________________

Name________________________________ Date________________

Paragraphs

The sentences below work together. They all talk about the same thing.

Sometimes directions are hard to read, but they help us do things. Reading directions can make life easier. It is easier to read hard directions than to live your life without looking at directions.

When a group of sentences work together, we call those sentences a **paragraph.**

The sentences below do not make a good paragraph. One sentence does not belong.

There are kits for putting white sidewalls on black tires. The kits are easy to use. You just put pieces of white rubber on the black tires. If you follow directions, the rubber will stay on the tire. I don't like pizza, though.

1. Copy the sentence that doesn't belong in the paragraph.

____

One sentence does not belong in the paragraph below.

Mary and her friends were going on a picnic. They wanted to be sure the car was in good shape. It might rain at the picnic. They decided to check the brakes and the oil. Susan said they should check the air in the tires, too.

2. Copy the sentence that doesn't belong.

____

Discussion

In each paragraph above, the first line is different from the other lines. How is it different? You **indent** the first line of a paragraph. What do you think *indent* means?

Writing Letters

Write a letter that has one paragraph. Tell a friend about going on a picnic.

1. Put your street address here. → ____________________

2. Put your city, state, and ZIP code here. ————————→ ____________________

3. Put today's date here. ——→ ____________________

4. Dear ______________, ←——— Put your friend's name here. Write the paragraph on the lines below.

5. ____

____

____

____

____

____

Your friend,

6. Sign your name here. ——→ ____________________

★ Using the Telephone Directory

Find the telephone number of a Laundromat. Look in the white pages. If you do not know a name, look under "Laundries" in the Yellow Pages.

Write the number here. ____________________

★ Using the Telephone

Show the class how you would call a Laundromat and ask when it is open.

Name______________________________ Date ____________

Proper Nouns

The names of the days of the week are proper nouns. They always start with capital letters.

Sunday Monday Tuesday Wednesday

Thursday Friday Saturday

Answer the questions.Start each name with a capital letter.

1. What day comes after Friday? ____________________

2. What day comes before Thursday? ____________________

3. It is Tuesday. What was yesterday? ____________________

4. It is Sunday. I will go to school tomorrow. What day will it be when I go to school? ____________________

5. Two days of the week are called the *weekend.* What days are they? ____________________ and ____________________

6. It is Wednesday. What was the day before yesterday?

____

7. It is Thursday. What is the day after tomorrow?

____

8. What day of the week has the longest name?

____

★ The Telephone Directory

Your telephone directory has directions on how to make a long-distance call. Find the information. Write it on a piece of paper.

★ Giving Directions

Tell the class how to make a long-distance call.

Writing Sentences

Write six sentences. Use the name of a day in each sentence. Use different days.

1. Sunday is my first day back to work

2. Thursday is my last day of work

3. I go to school on saturday

4. Everybody in my family goes to school or work on Monday

5. wednesday is called spagetti day

6. I do not like tuesday that much, it is a boring day

Word Puzzle

Six days of the week are hidden in this puzzle. Find them. Mark them like this:

W	S	A	D
E	A	V	Y
X	D	E	L

T	W	E	D	N	E	S	D	A	Y
T	S	S	T	A	D	A	E	U	S
H	A	D	A	Y	S	D	N	N	D
U	T	A	D	A	D	A	S	D	A
R	U	Y	U	M	O	N	D	A	Y
S	R	T	U	E	S	D	A	Y	S
D	D	A	D	D	A	Y	Y	H	T
A	A	D	A	F	R	I	D	A	Y
Y	Y	S	Y	S	A	T	R	D	A

Name ______________________ Date __________

Discussion

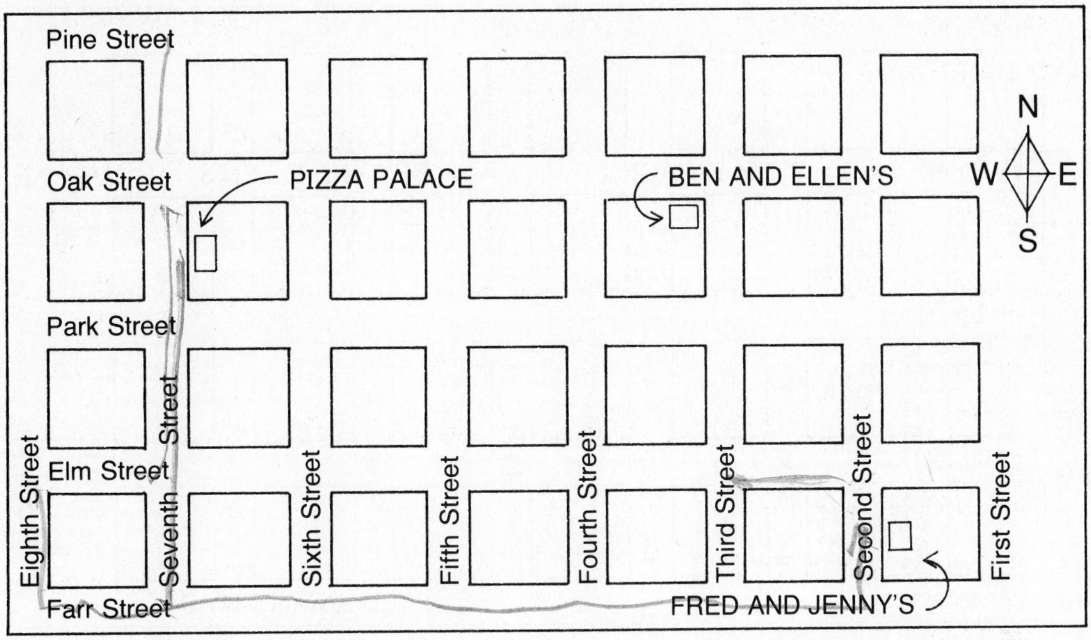

There are some letters just outside this map. What do the letters mean? Can you name two streets that run east and west? Can you name two streets that run north and south? Find the words *Pizza Palace.* What do the words and the arrow tell you? Why do people need maps?

Following Directions

1. Start at the corner of Elm Street and Second Street. Go one block west and two blocks north. Where are you?

____

2. Start at Eighth and Farr. Go six blocks east. Go one-half block north. Where are you? scond street

3. What street is two blocks north of Park Street? pine street

4. Start at the Pizza Palace. Go two and one-half blocks south. You are at seven street Street and far Street.

Writing Directions

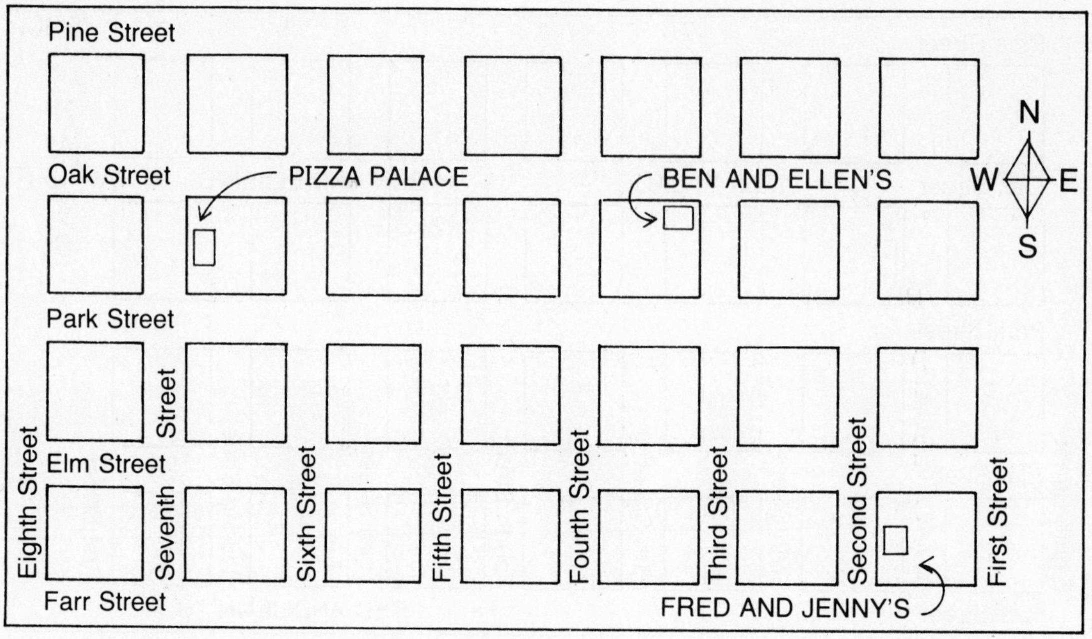

Jenny wrote these directions. They tell Ellen how to get to Jenny's house.

Go east to Second Street.
Go 2½ blocks south on Second.

1. Write directions for going from Ben and Ellen's to the Pizza Palace. go three and a half blocks w than turn half a block S on seventh street

2. Write directions for going from the Pizza Palace to Fred and Jenny's. Go two an half blocks S than you are going to find farr street, go five blocks E, turn N on second street and it is half a bla

3. Write directions for going from school to another place.

1

24

Name ______________________ Date ____________

End Punctuation

Put the correct punctuation mark at the end of each sentence.

1. Many things that you buy, come with a guarantee ___
   Do many things that you buy come with a guarantee ?
2. Do you know what a guarantee is ?
   I know what a guarantee is !
3. Is a guarantee the same thing as a warranty ?
   Oh, oh, that's not a guarantee !
   A guarantee is like a warranty !
4. A guarantee says that the brush you buy will work !
   Does a guarantee say that what you buy will work ?
   Ha, it says this brush will work !
5. Wow, I got a refund !
   If it doesn't work, you get a refund !
   Will you get a refund if it doesn't work ?

Completing Forms

Fill out this warranty card.

Name Eva Borges			
Address 71 Ashland St			
City Taunton	State Mass	ZIP 02780	
Dealer General Motors			
Date Purchased 6-28-86	Your Phone 8221193		

Reading Carefully

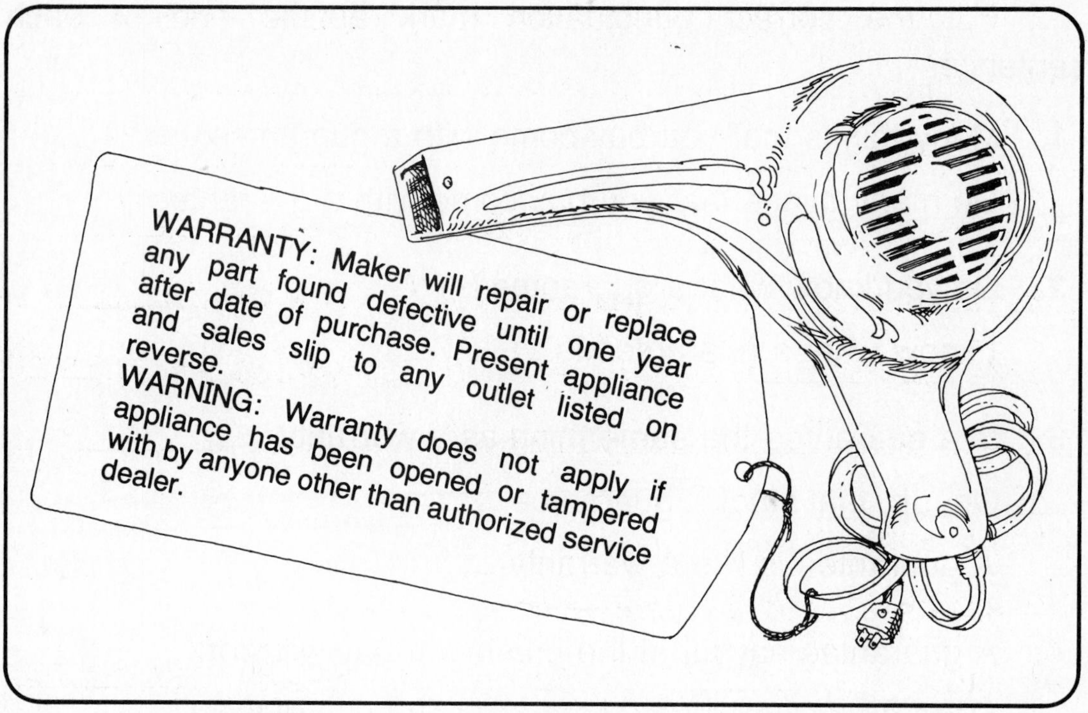
WARRANTY: Maker will repair or replace any part found defective until one year after date of purchase. Present appliance and sales slip to any outlet listed on reverse.
WARNING: Warranty does not apply if appliance has been opened or tampered with by anyone other than authorized service dealer.

A warranty says that if something doesn't work, the maker will fix it. Read the warranty above. Then answer these questions.

1. For how long will the maker repair or replace a part?

The maker will repair or replace a part until one year

2. The warranty says "present appliance and sales slip to any outlet listed on reverse." What does that mean? Put a line under the correct answer:

Take appliance and sales slip to any store shown on the back of this card.

This is a present. Turn it over.

3. If you try to fix the appliance yourself, is your warranty still good? No

4. What does "any part found defective" mean?

It means does not work

Name ______________________________ Date ______________

Using the Dictionary

Find each word in the dictionary. Copy the definition.

1. refund is

2. guarantee says that the article works and that it can be replaced if it doesn't work

3. replace means that you can have another one if it doesn't work

Writing Sentences

Use each word in a sentence.

4. guarantee is a prove the wath you bought is working and that can be replaced if it doesn't

5. replace is having a new part put in, instead of the defective one

6. refund is a reembars of the value of something if you are not satisfied with it

7. warranty is a statemente that tells you that if something doesn't work the company will fix it!

Proofreading

Check your work. Does each sentence make sense? Did you start each sentence with a capital letter? Did you end each sentence with the right punctuation?.

Abbreviations

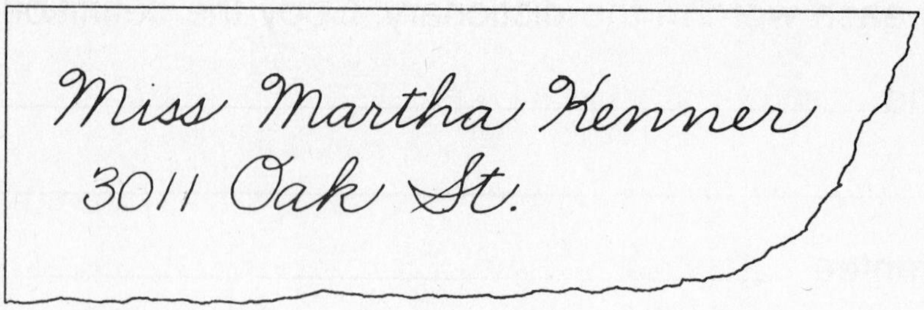

Many forms ask for your street address. You can use abbreviations for the street address. An abbreviation is a short way to write a word. You can use these abbreviations for four kinds of streets.

St. Street | Ave. Avenue

Blvd. Boulevard | Pl. Place

Write abbreviations for the streets below.

1. 3011 Oak Street St
2. 411 Swan Avenue Ave
3. 525 Ash Boulevard Blvd
4. 810 Adams Place Pl

Sometimes street addresses have a direction: East, West, North, or South. You can abbreviate the direction, too.

East Oak E. Oak | South Taylor S. Taylor

West Adams W. Adams | North Clay N. Clay

Use abbreviations for each address below.

5. 237 West Park Avenue 237 w park ave
6. 124 North Clay Boulevard 124 N Clay Blvd
7. 325 East Green Street 325 E Green St
8. 2011 South Main Street 2011 S Main St
9. 7777 East Key Boulevard 7777 E Key Blvd
10. 899 West Elm Avenue 899 w Elm St

Name_________________________________ Date ____________

Verbs

1. Find short words in each longer word below. Mark them like this: added

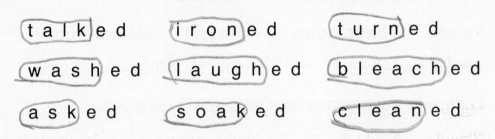

talked ironed turned

washed laughed bleached

asked soaked cleaned

2. Mark the short words in the longer words below.

talking ironing

washing laughing

asking soaking

The words you were working with are **verbs.** Verbs tell what happens. The longer verbs are made of short verbs with endings. The endings tell *when* something happens.

I **washed** my clothes yesterday. I am **washing** them now.

Use each word below in a sentence.

3. soaked my clothes yesterday

4. soaking I am soaking my clothes

5. bleached yesterday I bleached my clothes

6. bleaching I am bleaching my clothes

Verbs

Some verbs that tell about the past are tricky. If you don't say "have" or "has," you use one verb. If you do say "have" or "has," you use a different verb.

I **went.** I **have gone.** He **ran.** He **has run.**

She did the lesson. She **has done** the lesson.

Complete each sentence. Choose the right verb.

1. She has done. (went, gone)
2. She did to the car. (ran, run)
3. You do a good job. (did, done)
4. She has run the best race. (ran, run)
5. I have done my work. (did, done)
6. He has done that before. (did, done)
7. They went with us. (went, gone)
8. Who did that? (did, done)
9. The car ran smoothly. (ran, run)
10. My cat has run away. (ran, run)
11. We have done our best. (did, done)
12. They have gone on a trip. (went, gone)
13. They did the same thing last year. (did, done)
14. I went with them last year. (went, gone)
15. She did her work well. (did, done)

★ Speaking Carefully

Say each sentence aloud. Use the right verb.

Name ______________________________ Date ____________

Capitalization and Punctuation Review

Copy the sentences below. Put capital letters where they belong. Add the correct end punctuation.

1. the world is full of directions to read

The world is full of directions to read!

2. why are there so many directions

Why are there so many directions?

3. on sunday, monday, or any day, directions help you

On Sunday, Monday, or any day directions help you!

4. what happened when fred did not read directions

What happened when Fred did no read directions?

5. can you think of other directions

Can you think of other directions?

6. does this book have directions

Does this book have directions

Writing Sentences Review

7. Write a telling sentence. Use a person's name in your sentence.

Ana was very abset yesterday!

8. Write an asking sentence. Use a street name in your sentence.

Do you know if Joe lives on Ashland St?

Word Puzzle

1. Find these words in the puzzle: Mark them like this:

B	A	R	N	T	L
T	V	A	E	X	Y
O	A	N	G	R	Y
V	W	Y	X	O	L

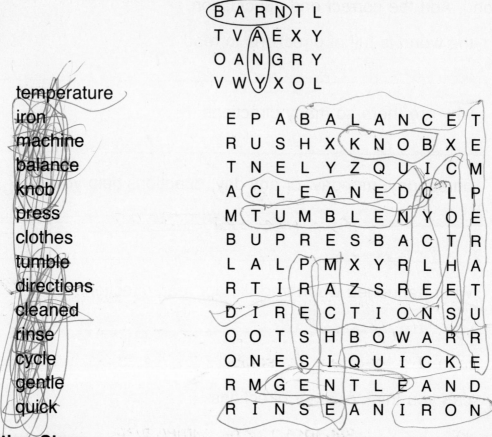

temperature
iron
machine
balance
knob
press
clothes
tumble
directions
cleaned
rinse
cycle
gentle
quick

E	P	A	B	A	L	A	N	C	E	T
R	U	S	H	X	K	N	O	B	X	E
T	N	E	L	Y	Z	Q	U	I	C	M
A	C	L	E	A	N	E	D	C	L	P
M	T	U	M	B	L	E	N	Y	O	E
B	U	P	R	E	S	B	A	C	T	R
L	A	L	P	M	X	Y	R	L	H	A
R	T	I	R	A	Z	S	R	E	E	T
D	I	R	E	C	T	I	O	N	S	U
O	O	T	S	H	B	O	W	A	R	R
O	N	E	S	I	Q	U	I	C	K	E
R	M	G	E	N	T	L	E	A	N	D
R	I	N	S	E	A	N	I	R	O	N

Writing Signs

2. Write your own sign. It can be serious or funny.

Name ______________________________ Date ______________

Chapter 3: WRITING LETTERS

Addresses: Titles

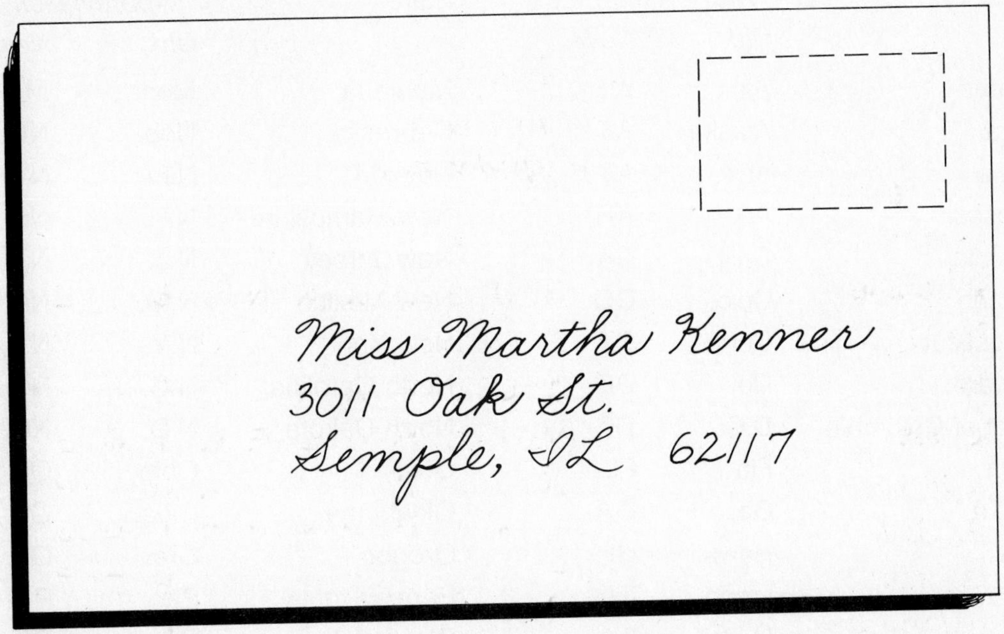

Look at the first line of the address. The first line shows the title and full name. Here are some of the titles used in addresses:

Title	*Use*
Mr.	Used for single or married men
Miss	Used for single women
Mrs.	Used for married women
Ms.	Used for single or married women
Dr.	Used for doctors

Put the correct title before each name below.

1. __________ George Brown (single)

2. __________ Lilly Bolo (single)

3. __________ Carol Chouteau (married)

4. __________ Robert Towns (married)

5. __________ Eve Nagoti (you don't know whether she's married or not)

Abbreviations: States

State	Abbreviation Old	New
Alabama	Ala.	AL
Alaska	Alaska	AK
Arizona	Ariz.	AZ
Arkansas	Ark.	AR
California	Calif.	CA
Colorado	Colo.	CO
Connecticut	Conn.	CT
Delaware	Del.	DE
District of Columbia	D.C.	DC
Florida	Fla.	FL
Georgia	Ga.	GA
Hawaii	Hawaii	HI
Idaho	Idaho	ID
Illinois	Ill.	IL
Indiana	Ind.	IN
Iowa	Iowa	IA
Kansas	Kans.	KS
Kentucky	Ky.	KY
Louisiana	La.	LA
Maine	Me.	ME
Maryland	Md.	MD
Massachusetts	Mass.	MA
Michigan	Mich.	MI
Minnesota	Minn.	MN
Mississippi	Miss.	MS
Missouri	Mo.	MO

State	Abbreviation Old	New
Montana	Mont.	MT
Nebraska	Neb.	NE
Nevada	Nev.	NV
New Hampshire	N.H.	NH
New Jersey	N.J.	NJ
New Mexico	N.M.	NM
New York	N.Y.	NY
North Carolina	N.C.	NC
North Dakota	N.D.	ND
Ohio	Ohio	OH
Oklahoma	Okla.	OK
Oregon	Ore.	OR
Pennsylvania	Pa.	PA
Rhode Island	R.I.	RI
South Carolina	S.C.	SC
South Dakota	S.Dak.	SD
Tennessee	Tenn.	TN
Texas	Tex.	TX
Utah	Utah	UT
Vermont	Vt.	VT
Virginia	Va.	VA
Washington	Wash.	WA
West Virginia	W. Va.	WV
Wisconsin	Wis.	WI
Wyoming	Wyo.	WY

The chart above shows abbreviations for the states. It shows the old abbreviations and the new Post Office abbreviations.

Write the new abbreviation for each state below.

1. Ohio OH

2. Utah UT

3. Maine Me

4. Iowa IA

Name ______________________ Date ____________

Addresses

This mark is a **comma:** **,** We put a comma between the name of a city and the name of the state.

Add commas and periods to these addresses.

1. Miss Helen Alonzo
34 W Ave,
Bamer IA 66789

2. Mrs Mary Tam
452 Cross St
Cann, CA 99876

3. Mr John White
80665 Bend Blvd,
Blintown PA 44367

4. Mr Leroy Brown
1234 Links Pl
Leesburg, OH 43265

Write the addresses for the people below. Use the new state abbreviations. Put capital letters where they belong.

5. edward amory lives at 2334 oak street in latitia, new york. His ZIP code is 11110.

Edward Amory lives at 2334 oak street, in Leatitia, New York His zip cod is 11110

6. ferna foy lives at 47 forge place in linden, texas. Her ZIP code is 77700.

Ferna Foy lives at 47 Forge Place in linden, Texas Her ZIP cod is 77700

Commas in Sentences

Add commas to these sentences.

7. Mr. Robert Bunting lives in Barden, Vermont.

8. Mr. Bunting's friend lives in King, Tennessee.

9. Are King, Tennessee, and Barden, Vermont, in the same state? No

10. Do you live in Arlington, Mississippi? No

11. Does Mr. Bunting live in Chicago, Illinois? No

Addressing Envelopes

We use two addresses on envelopes. The address in the middle of the envelope shows who gets the letter. The address in the upper left-hand corner tells who sent the letter. This address is called the return address.

The middle address above has an extra line. It tells the name of a school as well as the name of a person.

1. Copy the address of the person who will get the letter.

2. Copy the address of the person who sent the letter.

Name ______________________ Date ____________

Addressing Envelopes

Address envelope 1 to Mrs. Agnes Citie, Rite Cafe, 466 Main Street, Jay, New York 10009. Address envelope 2 to Mr. Walter Groff, 17 Canyon Street, Lianta, Utah 11118. Use your return address for both envelopes. Use abbreviations.

1.

2.

Maze

Find the path of the letter. *Hint:* It has to go to the post office before it is delivered.

Name ______________________ Date ____________

Business Letter Form

Heading → 26 North Fourth Ave.
Wilton, NY 11101
August 11, 19__

Ms. Mildred Kneebler
Ace Trade School
2601 Main St.
Wilton, NY 11103
← Inside Address

Dear Ms. Kneebler: ← Greeting

Thank you for helping me find my new job. I would never have found such a good job if you had not helped me.

Body

Closing → Sincerely,

Signature → *Elton Alden*
Elton Alden

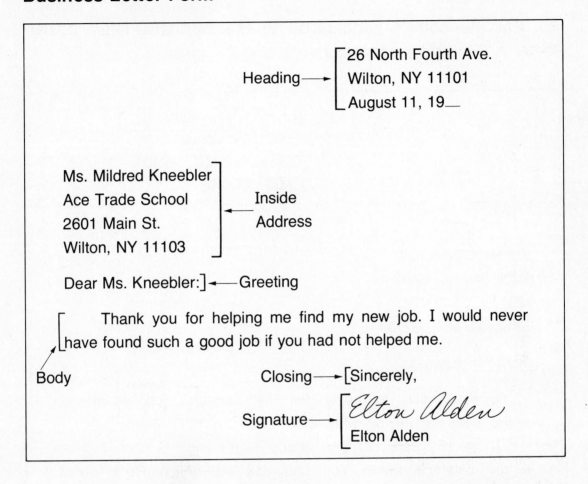

Look at the parts of the letter above carefully. Use this letter to answer the questions below.

1. The *envelope* ______ shows the address of the person who sent the letter.

2. The date is a part of the ______________.

3. What part shows who got the letter? *Middle* ______________

4. The punctuation mark after the greeting of a business letter is called a **colon.** What punctuation mark is used after the closing?

____

5. What punctuation mark is used after the greeting? ______________

6. How many times is a comma used? ______________

Business Letters

1. Put the correct punctuation in the business letter below. Remember to add the four commas and the colon.

1821 W Jones St
Elmwood MO 62131
May 21 19___

Mr John Edwards
Black Mower Company
123 Fir St
Elmwood MO 62134

Dear Mr Edwards

I would like to apply for the cafeteria job advertised in the *Daily Globe* on May 20.

I am 16 years old and attend North High School. I work in the cafeteria there. You can ask Mrs Alice Rock about my work.

If you would like to interview me, you can reach me at 812-3640.

Sincerely

Leroy Webb

Leroy Webb

2. Pretend that you are Mr. Edwards. Write an answer to Leroy Webb. You want him to come to your office for an interview at 4:00 P.M. on May 29. Use a separate sheet of paper for your letter.

Name ______________________ Date ____________

Friendly Letters

Heading → 231 Hillview Lane
Elmtown, NJ 02096
June 30, 19__

Dear Angie, ← Greeting

I am glad to hear that you are happy in your new home. We miss you, but I look forward to seeing you this Christmas.

Body

Closing → As ever,

Signature → Joe

The letter above is called a *friendly letter.*

1. Does a friendly letter have a heading? yes
2. Does a friendly letter have an inside address? No
3. What punctuation mark follows the greeting? ,
4. Put the correct punctuation in the friendly letter below.

357 W First St
Ashtown MN 45782
July 18 19__

Dear Ethel

Thank you for the beautiful flowers. It was so nice of you to remember that blue is my favorite color!

Love

Belinda

Business Letters

1. Punctuate the business letter below.

> 642 Benton Sq
> Amity NE 78542
> May 4 19__
>
> Mr Charles Stone
> 2888 W Green St
> New Hope, RI 86321
>
> Dear Mr Stone
>
> Thank you for your letter of April 30, requesting an appointment for May 26. Unfortunately, I will be out of town that day. Could you call on the afternoon of May 27?
>
> Sincerely yours
> *Agnes Malone*
> Agnes Malone

2. Pretend that you are Mr. Charles Stone. Write to Ms. Agnes Malone. Tell her that you accept her invitation to call on the afternoon of May 27. Use a separate sheet of paper.

3. Draw an envelope. Address it to Ms. Agnes Malone. Use Mr. Charles Stone's return address.

★ Using the Telephone

Work with a friend. Pretend that you are Charles Stone. Call Agnes Malone. Ask for an appointment. Act out what each of you would say.

Name ______________________ Date ____________

Friendly Letters

Punctuate the friendly letters below.

7650 Ash St
Linwood MN 45872
July 15 19__

Dear Ellie

I hope you can come to visit us soon. Everybody in the family, wants to know when their favorite lady, will be coming to town. I really look forward to seeing you.

Love
Bert

---

11 Aldrich Ave
Eventown MN 45742
July 29 19__

Dear Bert

Your letter made me want to see you very much. I can come next Saturday and stay until Wednesday. Please write, and tell me, whether this is all right with you. I can't wait!

Love
Ellie

★ Writing Letters

Pretend that you are Bert. Write an answer to Ellie.

Writing Friendly Letters

Write a letter with one paragraph. Tell what you did before you came to school this morning.

★ Giving Directions

Plan to tell your classmates how to get to a certain place. Make sure you know the directions yourself. Tell the directions in the right order. Speak clearly.

Name ______________________________ Date ____________

Verbs

Read the sentences below. Say them softly to yourself. Put a ring around the verb that sounds right.

1. Ann (choosed, chose) to play.
2. We (drank, drunk) two glasses each.
3. We have (drove, driven) there many times.
4. Maggie has (eaten, ate) there before.
5. They have (forgot, forgotten) the money.
6. I never (heared, heard) the bell.
7. Whatever (became, become) of the president?
8. The glass is (broke, broken).
9. I have (rode, ridden) that horse.
10. He has (wrote, written) that letter.
11. I (give, gave) him all I could.
12. It was (tore, torn) off.
13. She (did, done) the best job.
14. The car has (fell, fallen) into the ditch.
15. They (sung, sang) my favorite songs.
16. I (saw, seen) it last night.

Sometimes a verb has a helping verb. Here are some of the verbs that can be helping verbs: *has, had, have, was, were, is, are.*

I **go** to school. I **have gone** to school.

17. Eight of the exercises above have helping verbs. Find the helping verbs. Draw a line under them.

Pronouns

Read the sentences below. Say each sentence softly to yourself. Put a ring around the pronoun that sounds right.

1. I will do it for you and (he, him).
2. They asked (he, him) to be on the team.
3. May (me and Joe, Joe and I) go with her?
4. It must have been for (we, us).
5. (Her, She) likes it.
6. (We, Us) girls had not been there.
7. Did you want (her, she) to call?
8. Between you and (I, me), I'm scared.
9. (We, Us) were the ones who called.
10. Did he ask (us, we) boys?
11. (Me and Al, Al and I) like it.
12. It sounds like (her, she).
13. Don't let (him, he) do it.
14. They met (Luke and me, me and Luke) at the rodeo.
15. (Me and you, You and I) should go.
16. Did you tell (she, her)?
17. (She, Her) left town.

★ Speaking Carefully

Read the sentences aloud. Use the right pronoun. Choose five pronouns. Make up your own sentences, using those pronouns. Read your sentences to the class. Listen to sentences that others read. Were the pronouns used correctly?

Name ______________________________ Date ____________

Recognizing Paragraphs

In a paragraph, all the sentences tell about the same thing. Usually, the first line of a paragraph is indented.

1. The sentences below look like one paragraph, but they should be two paragraphs. Find the sentence that should start a new paragraph. Draw a line under that sentence.

> The first clock that people used was the sun. By seeing where the sun was in the sky people could tell whether it was morning or afternoon. Atomic clocks are very accurate. Some atomic clocks could run for 3,000 years and only lose one second. Atomic clocks are very expensive.

2. Find the sentence that should start a new paragraph. Draw a line under that sentence.

> Some insects have strong legs. They can jump very far. A flea can jump far. A grasshopper is a strong jumper. Spiders make webs to catch insects. There are many kinds of webs. Different kinds of spiders make different webs.

3. Copy the second paragraph of exercise 2.

____

____

____

____

____

★ Using the Library

Go to the library. Find some more information about spiders. Write a paragraph about what you learn.

Writing Paragraphs

The sentences below are all mixed up. If they are put together right, they will make two paragraphs. Rewrite the sentences to make two paragraphs. Remember to indent the first line of each paragraph.

There are many unusual homes around the world. Homes can be made of grass. One kind of clock used long ago was a candle clock. A candle clock told time by the length of time it took to burn down. Homes can be made from blocks of ice. An hour candle would burn down in one hour. Homes can be made from paper. Almost anything you can think of can be used to make a home.

Name ______________________________ Date ______________

Writing Friendly Letters

Write a letter that has two paragraphs. Tell about something you did yesterday in the first paragraph. In the second paragraph, tell about something you hope you can do tomorrow.

Abbreviations

Rewrite the addresses below. Use abbreviations for directions, streets, and states. Use commas and periods where needed.

1. Mrs Philippa Fogg ______________________
   34 Alton Avenue ______________________
   Marian Ohio 55544 ______________________

2. Miss Alverina Abgado ______________________
   4557 West Pleasant Place ______________________
   Dormont Delaware 11111 ______________________

3. Ms Emilia Abbie ______________________
   Acme Tire Sales ______________________
   3456 West Main Street ______________________
   Pardon Wyoming 64432 ______________________

4. Mr Lathrop Richmann ______________________
   6 Buff Boulevard ______________________
   Falls Vermont 00099 ______________________

5. Mr Gordon Lightly ______________________
   5677 Darner Place ______________________
   Diener Utah 64444 ______________________

6. Mr Leo Brown ______________________
   78809 East Tam Boulevard ______________________
   Wilton Arkansas 01111 ______________________

Name ______________________________ Date ______________

Reading Carefully

Mahatma Tool Co.
34 Indira Ave.
Falls Church, VA 22234
June 15, 19__

Mrs. Ann Ashner
45 First Ave.
Falls Church, VA 22236

Dear Mrs. Ashner:

Enclosed is the employment application form that you asked for on the telephone yesterday.

Sincerely,

Burke Bogess

Burke Bogess

Read the letter above. Then answer each question below.

1. What did Mr. Bogess send to Ann? ______________________________

____

2. How did Mr. Bogess know Ann wanted it? ______________________

____

★ Writing Letters

Pretend you are Ann. On a separate sheet of paper, write to Mr. Bogess. Let him know that you got the application form. Tell him you will call for an interview as soon as you have the form ready.

Writing Business Letters

Write a letter with one paragraph. Pretend you are asking Mrs. Pauline Gertz for an appointment to talk about a job. Tell Mrs. Gertz that you can come at any time that she has free.

Mrs. Pauline Gertz
City Supply Co.
123 W. Fourth St.
Mintown, NM 84523

Dear Mrs. Gertz:

★ **Using the Telephone**

Call your local post office. Find out how much it costs to mail a regular-size birthday card to France. Write the information.

Name ______________________________ Date ____________

Writing Business Letters

Pretend that you saw Mrs. Gertz last Wednesday. She told you that you have the job. You will start next week. Write a letter with one paragraph. Thank Mrs. Gertz for her help.

★ Writing Letters

Write a letter to the editor of your local newspaper. Write about something that you saw in the newspaper last week.

Punctuation Review

Add commas, periods, and colons to the letter. Circle every word or abbreviation that should start with a capital letter.

11 lawton blvd
taylorville tx 77765
may 17 19__

mr artemis woodruff
central states tire co
45 parkway place
taylorville tx 77733

dear mr woodruff

thank you for taking the time to speak with me yesterday i enjoyed meeting you and learning about the requirements for jobs at central states tire company. i hope you agree that i would be a good salesperson i look forward to hearing from you in the near future. if i have not heard from you by Wednesday, may 28, may i call to see whether the job is still open?

sincerely

★ Writing Letters

Write a letter to your teacher. Tell your teacher some things that you like about the school. Tell some things that you think can be changed. Use the school address.

Name ______________________________ Date ______________

Business Letter Review

Mr. Eli Baldwin wants to talk to you about a job in his restaurant. He wants you to meet him there at 3:30 P.M. next Tuesday, April 17. His address is Service Cafe, 911 Orange Street, Fairview, Virginia 33345.

Write an answer to Mr. Baldwin. Use your own address.

Verbs Review

Read the sentences below. Say them softly to yourself. Then circle the verb that sounds right.

1. Was your money (took, taken)?
2. Ellen (brung, brought) me the bill.
3. Who could have (stole, stolen) it?
4. Alex (wrote, written) the note.
5. Last week Ann (gave, give) me a new one.
6. Our car was (stole, stolen).
7. Has he (ate, eaten) it all?
8. Ruth and Luke have (gone, went) to the game.
9. Mother (seen, saw) the fire.
10. She has (took, taken) a chance.
11. He (saw, seen) the fight last night.
12. The child had (growed, grown) six inches.
13. Clyde has (gone, went) to the office.
14. Has the water (frozen, froze)?

Use each verb in a sentence: did done went gone

15. The kids did their home work
16. I have done all I could
17. Stille went to school yesterday
18. Thei have gone to far

★ Speaking Carefully

Read each sentence above aloud.

Name ________________________________ Date ____________

Pronouns Review

Read the sentences below. Say them softly to yourself. Circle the pronoun that sounds right.

1. Let's tell on (they, them).
2. (They, Them) broke it.
3. It must have been for (they, them).
4. It wasn't for (us, we).
5. We knew (him, he) would do that.
6. Ask Jane and (he, him) to do the work.
7. (Bill and I, Me and Bill) don't see anyone.
8. John and (he, him) were ready.
9. Don't say a word about it to (she, her).
10. (Me and him, He and I) will quit.
11. Come with (we, us).
12. Mary plays chess with (I, me).
13. Divide it between Larry and (he, him).
14. Carol must have been with (she, her).
15. (He, Him) and Alice left together.

★ Speaking Carefully

Read the sentences above aloud. Make up a sentence for each of these pronouns.

he	we	them	I	me
she	they	her	him	

Say your sentences to the class.

Making Puzzles

1. You can make a puzzle. Hide the words below in the squares. Give the puzzle to a friend. See whether the friend can find the words. Try to find the words in your friend's puzzle.

package	office	address	return
title	state	single	married

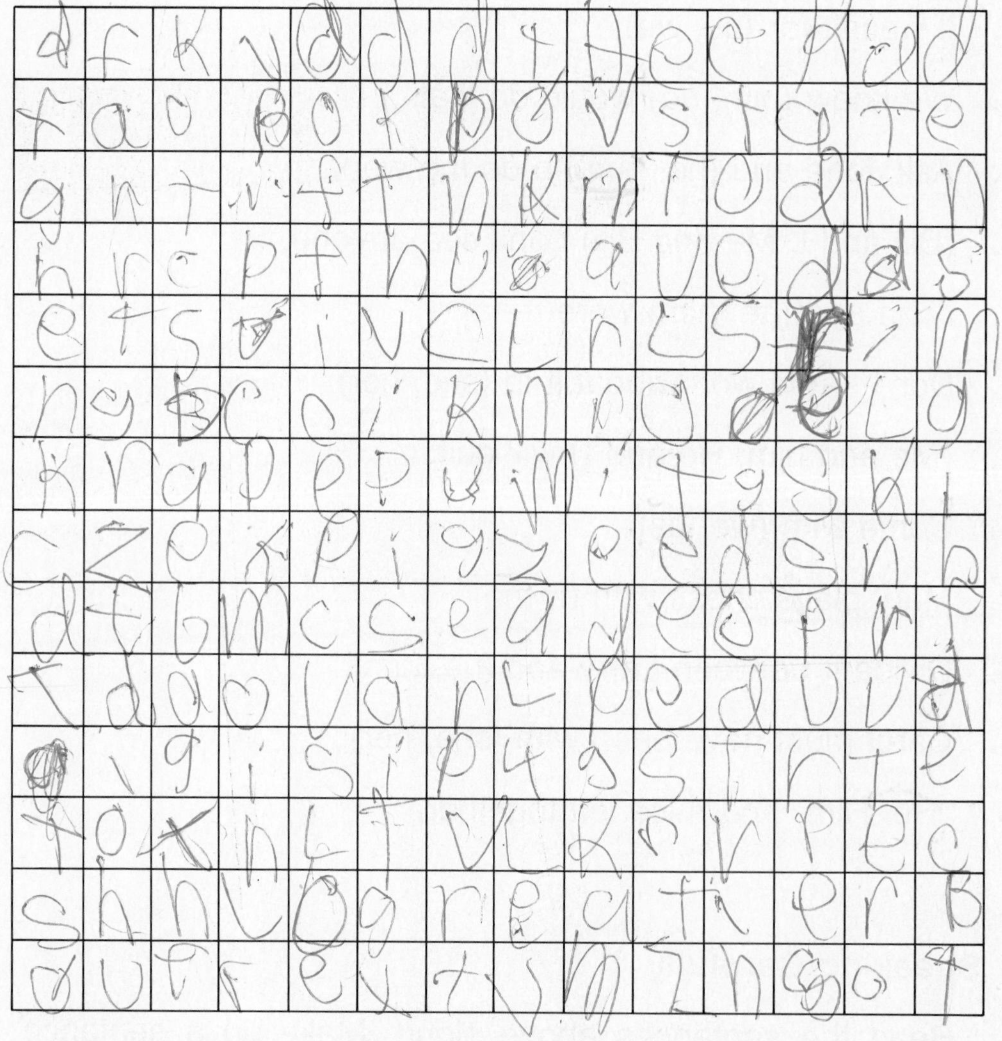

2. Make your own puzzle. Copy the squares above. Use these words.

abbreviation	punctuation	business	greeting
sincerely	signature	closing	heading

Name ______________________ Date ____________

Chapter 4: UNDERSTANDING SIGNS

Discussion

Thousands of people are killed because they do not obey traffic signs. What might happen if you did not see the "men working" sign? What could happen if you did not obey the detour sign? What might happen if you went the wrong way on a one-way street?

Writing Sentences

Write three sentences. In each sentence, tell something about a traffic sign. Tell what it means or why it is important.

1. ____

____

2. ____

____

3. ____

____

The Dictionary

merge (mėrj) *v.* **1.** To swallow up, combine, or absorb: *The two companies were merged into the giant corporation.* **2.** To blend together without sudden change: *The traffic was merging smoothly until the accident.*

yield (yēld) *v.* **1.** To produce: *The ocean yields many fish.* **2.** To give up: *I yield to your wishes.*

Read the dictionary entries. Then answer the exercises below.

Sometimes a dictionary gives more than one definition of a word. The definitions are numbered. Copy the two definitions of *merge.*

1. ______________________________

2. ______________________________

The definitions above also give example sentences. The example sentences are in slanted type. Copy the two example sentences for *yield.*

3. ______________________________

4. ______________________________

You may see traffic signs that say, "Merge." Copy the definition of *merge* that fits these signs.

5. ______________________________

Copy the definition of *yield* that fits the yield signs.

6. ______________________________

Writing Sentences

Use one of the words in a sentence.

7. ______________________________

Name ______________________ Date ____________

Reading Signs

Write a sentence to tell what each sign means. For example:

Trains cross here.

1. ______________________________

____

2. ______________________________

____

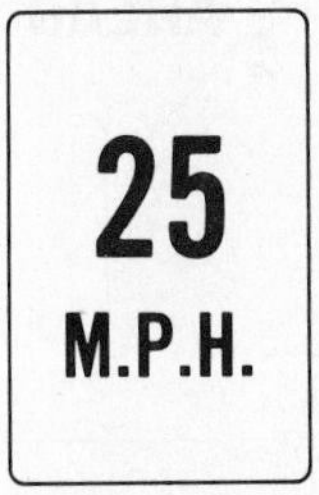

3. ______________________________

____

4. ______________________________

____

5. ______________________________

____

Reading Signs

Write sentences to tell what each sign means.

1. ______________________________

2. ______________________________

3. ______________________________

4. ______________________________

5. ______________________________

6. ______________________________

7. ______________________________

Name ______________________________ Date ____________

Noun Plurals

Some nouns name one thing: *sign, noun, letter.* Some nouns name more than one thing: *signs, nouns, letters.* Nouns that name more than one thing are called **plural nouns.** Most plural nouns end with *s.*

Nouns	*Plural Nouns*	*Nouns*	*Plural Nouns*
car	cars	street	streets
boy	boys	girl	girls

Here are some nouns. Change each one to a plural noun. Add an *s* to each one.

1. student ______________ **2.** school ______________

3. room ______________ **4.** license ______________

5. lesson ______________ **6.** teacher ______________

7. day ______________ **8.** night ______________

9. dollar ______________ **10.** cent ______________

Some plural nouns do not end with *s.* Some nouns change their spelling for the plural. Can you write the plural for these nouns?

11. man ______________ **12.** woman ______________

13. foot ______________ **14.** child ______________

Some plural nouns end with *es.*

address	address**es**	bypass	bypass**es**

Write the correct plural for each noun below.

15. mess ______________ **16.** address ______________

17. guess ______________ **18.** bypass ______________

Noun Plurals

Complete each sentence below. Use the correct form of the noun.

1. Ten ________________ are in school. (child, children)
2. One ________________ is at the corner. (child, children)
3. Two ________________ are near the child. (man, men)
4. One ________________ tells the child to be careful. (man, men)
5. A ________________ sells you things. (store, stores)
6. An ________________ tells where people live. (address, addresses)
7. A ________________ helps you learn your lessons. (teacher, teachers)
8. Your ________________ help you stand up. (foot, feet)
9. Some ________________ help each other. (woman, women)
10. Some ________________ help you drive carefully. (sign, signs)

Nouns in Sentences

Add a noun to complete each sentence below. Use any naming word that works.

11. The ________________ runs fast.
12. The ________________ smells good.
13. Many ________________ live in that town.
14. Most ________________ like pizza.
15. The ________________ is yellow.

Name ______________________ Date __________

Abbreviations

Look at the picture. Find two abbreviations. Write them. Write what they mean.

1. ______________________

2. ______________________

inch or inches	in or ″	pound or pounds	lb
foot or feet	ft or ′	gallon or gallons	gal
yard or yards	yd	pint or pints	pt
mile or miles	mi	quart or quarts	qt
miles per hour	mph	ounce or ounces	oz

Read the abbreviations for measurements. Then write each measurement below the short way. Use abbreviations and numerals.

3. five feet seven inches ______________

4. twelve pounds six ounces ______________

5. twenty-five miles per hour ______________

6. one hundred yards ______________

7. one hundred and twenty-five pounds ______________

8. ten gallons ______________

Days and Months

Here are the abbreviations for days and months.

Sunday	Sun.	January	Jan.	July	—
Monday	Mon.	February	Feb.	August	Aug.
Tuesday	Tues.	March	Mar.	September	Sept.
Wednesday	Wed.	April	Apr.	October	Oct.
Thursday	Thurs.	May	—	November	Nov.
Friday	Fri.	June	—	December	Dec.
Saturday	Sat.				

Write the abbreviation for each word.

1. Saturday ____________ **2.** March ____________

3. Sunday ____________ **4.** October ____________

5. Wednesday ____________ **6.** August ____________

7. Thursday ____________ **8.** February ____________

9. Friday ____________ **10.** November ____________

11. Tuesday ____________ **12.** September ____________

13. Monday ____________ **14.** January ____________

Sometimes days and months can be written as numbers.

July 4, 1976 ——→ 7/4/76

Write these dates as numbers.

15. January 2, 1999 ____________

16. December 25, 1925 ____________

17. March 31, 1942 ____________

Name ______________________________ Date ______________

Alphabetical Order

In some words below, a short word is in a longer word. In alphabetical order, the short word goes first. Put the words below into alphabetical order.

1. laugh laughed black blacker

____

____

____

____

2. direction direct grand grandfather

____

____

____

____

3. safety safe sign signal railroads railroad

____

____

____

____

____

____

4. situate sit songs song songster songsters

____

____

____

____

____

____

5. crossing cross crossings crosses

____

____

____

____

6. drive drivers driving driver

____

____

____

____

Finding Sentences

Find the sentences in the four paragraphs below. Circle each word that should start with a capital letter. Add the correct end punctuation.

1. traffic signs are important every state spends a lot of money on traffic signs drivers should be able to read the signs drivers may have an accident if they cannot read the signs

2. some people read slowly they cannot read every sign they should remember the shape and color of each sign

3. slow down before you get to a stop sign you should not stop suddenly you can hurt the people in your car if you stop too fast do you know why

4. do not pass other cars on hills or curves do not pass other cars when you cannot see what is coming you could cause a head-on crash by passing in a no-passing zone don't ever cause a head-on crash

Writing Paragraphs

Write a paragraph. Tell three things that could happen if you drive carelessly.

5. ____

____

____

____

____

Name ________________________________ Date ______________

Discussion

The traffic signs in the pictures help people stay safe. Do you see signs for drivers? Are there signs for people who are walking? Are there people who cannot read the signs? What could happen to these people?

Writing Paragraphs

Look at the pictures carefully. One person is in danger. Find that person. Write a paragraph. Tell who the person is. Tell what kind of danger the person is in. Tell why the person is in danger.

____

____

____

____

____

Reading Maps

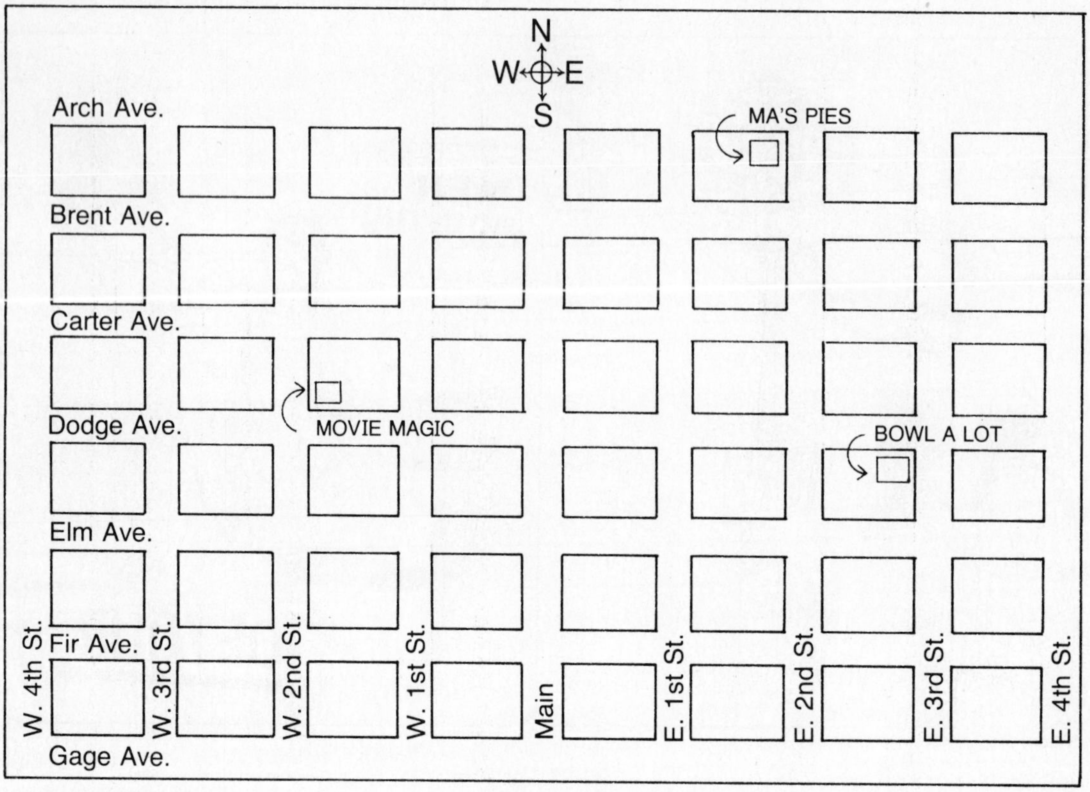

Look at the map. See how you would go from one place to another.

To go from Main and Elm to Bowl A Lot: Go north on Main to Dodge. Turn right on Dodge to Bowl A Lot.

Watch the arrows that show north, south, east, and west.

Pretend that you are at 443 E. Fir. You want to go to Ma's Pies. Tell how you would get there. Tell the streets you would take. Tell which way you would turn.

Name ______________________________ Date ______________

Reading Maps

Use the map on page 80 to answer these exercises.

1. You are at 443 E. Fir. You want to go to Movie Magic. Tell how you would get there.

____

____

____

2. You live at 210 W. Fir. You want to pick up your friend at 237 E. Arch.

____

____

____

3. You want to go from 237 E. Arch to Bowl A Lot.

____

____

____

4. You want to go back to 237 E. Arch.

____

____

____

5. You want to go from 237 E. Arch to 210 W. Fir.

____

____

____

____

Recognizing Sentences

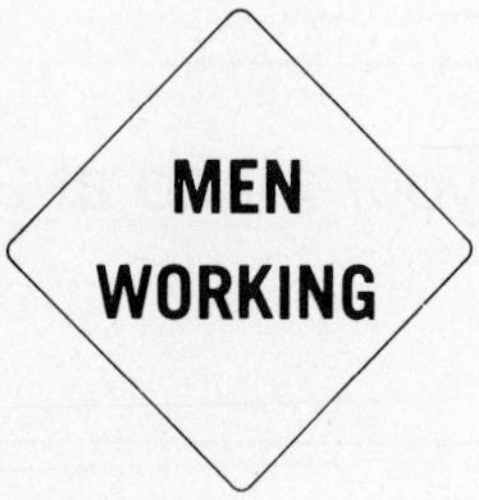

Read the groups of words below. Some are sentences. Some are not. Draw a line through the groups that are not sentences. Add the correct end punctuation to the real sentences.

1. What does a yellow light mean___
2. It means that you should get ready to stop___
3. Lots of people yellow lights___
4. Some of them green lights___
5. Do you know what green lights mean___
6. Do you know what a flashing light means___
7. Does a flashing light mean slow down___
8. You don't go at a red light___
9. Some signs are just for driving___
10. One sign tells you to merge___
11. What does *merge* mean___
12. Drivers in one lane must join drivers in the other lane___

Name ______________________ Date ____________

Writing Sentences

The groups of words below are not sentences. Rewrite them to make sentences. Add words.

1. signs in Laundromats washers and dryers

2. signs in airports tell you how your airplane

3. can signs in office buildings tell talk to someone job

4. your step

5. some signs hard, ugly, and small

6. if can't read a, what should do

7. you should "do not enter" sign

★ Explanations

Look in stores and other places. Find five signs that are not traffic signs.

Tell the class where the signs are. Tell what they say. Tell what they mean.

Discussion

The groups of words below are not sentences. They do not have *verbs.*

Joan the left turn arrow   Billy the car

A verb tells about doing something. Read the sentences below. Can you find a verb that tells what Joan did? What verb tells what Billy did?

Joan saw the left turn arrow.

Billy drove the car.

Can you think of other verbs that you could use in the sentence about Billy? Would these words work?

wrecked   washed   liked

Using Verbs

Add a verb to each group of words below. You may also add other words. Be sure to make a complete sentence.

1. Jenny ________________ the street.
2. She ________________ the stop sign.
3. Art ________________ the car.
4. He ________________ into Elm Street.
5. He ________________ the sign.
6. The sign ________________ "Do not enter."
7. The car ________________ through the stop sign.
8. Bill was ________________ the car.
9. He did not ________________ the stop sign.
10. The policeman ________________ him.

Name ______________________________ Date ______________

Using Verbs

Complete each set of sentences below in three different ways. Do this by using a different verb in each sentence.

Anna *threw* the ball.
Anna *kicked* the ball.
Anna *dropped* the ball.

1. Luke ______________________ the dog.
   Luke ______________________ the dog.
   Luke ______________________ the dog.
2. Tomorrow I will ______________________ the car.
   Tomorrow I will ______________________ the car.
   Tomorrow I will ______________________ the car.
3. Ruth ______________________ fast.
   Ruth ______________________ fast.
   Ruth ______________________ fast.
4. He ______________________ to town.
   He ______________________ to town.
   He ______________________ to town.

Change these verbs. One has been done for you.

5. I will go. I *went*. I have *gone*.
6. I see. I __________. I have __________.
7. I do. I __________. I have __________.
8. I run. I __________. I have __________.

Writing Sentences

Use each word in a sentence. Use the word as a verb.

1. fight (*or* fought)

____

2. catch (*or* caught)

____

3. kick (*or* kicked)

____

4. ride (*or* rode)

____

5. do (*or* did)

____

6. walk (*or* walked)

____

7. hear (*or* heard)

____

★ Understanding Verbs

Write a sentence or two. Explain the difference between the two sets of verbs below.

fight	do	fought	did
kick	walk	kicked	walked

★ Speaking Carefully

Read each of your sentences aloud. Speak clearly.

Name ________________________________ Date ____________

Writing Sentences

Write sentences. Tell what each sign means. One sentence has been written for you.

1. *Let the other cars go first.*

2. ________________________________

____

3. ________________________________

____

4. ________________________________

____

5. ________________________________

____

Proofreading

Check your work. Did you write complete sentences? Did you start each sentence with a capital letter? Did you end each sentence with the correct punctuation mark?

Discussion

Look at the picture. What signs do you see? Why is each sign important? How might each sign save your life? Can you think of other signs that can save your life?

Writing Paragraphs

Write a paragraph. Tell about a sign that can save your life. Tell why the sign is important.

____

____

____

____

____

Proofreading

Check your work. Do all your sentences work together? Is each sentence complete? Did you indent the first line?

Name ______________________________ Date ______________

Recognizing Sentences Review

Find the sentences in the paragraphs below. Circle each word that should start with a capital letter. Add the correct end punctuation.

1. do you know what to do when you see a detour sign you will have to drive on a different road you will have to follow many signs they tell you where the detour goes sometimes people get lost on detours watch carefully for the signs you should drive slowly when you are on a detour

2. traffic signs are important for people who drive cars traffic signs are important for people who do not drive, too they help people who are walking they help people who are riding bicycles they help people who are on motorcycles can you think of some reasons why traffic signs help people do the signs help keep people from getting hurt

3. most cities have rules about making U-turns there are signs on many big streets the signs tell drivers not to make U-turns do you know what a U-turn is do you know why there are laws against making one

4. many important signs are not traffic signs signs can be found in gas stations, libraries, offices, and schools some signs tell you where the entrance is some tell you where the exit is do some signs tell where the fire escape is do you know what a fire escape is for

Writing Paragraphs Review

1. Write a paragraph. Name the most important thing you learned in this chapter. Then give two reasons why it is important.

2. Write a paragraph. Name some of the important signs inside your school. Tell why these signs are important.

3. If you could put up a big sign in front of your school, what would it say? Tell what the sign would say. Write some reasons why you would make that sign.

Name ______________________________ Date ____________

Reading Signs Review

Read each description of a sign. Then write the word or words that belong on the sign. Here is an example:

You will have to drive on a different road. You cannot keep going on this one. *Detour*

1. You can drive only one way on this street. ____________
2. Here is where you leave. ____________
3. You cannot drive faster than 25 miles per hour. ____________
4. Do not go fast. ____________
5. Let other cars go before you do. ____________
6. Do not cross the street now. ____________
7. You can cross the street now. ____________
8. People are working on the street. ____________
9. You cannot park your car here. ____________
10. You cannot make a right turn here.

____

11. You cannot make a U-turn on this street.

____

12. Do not drive onto this street.

____

13. To go to Baker Park, get off at the next exit.

____

Verbs Review

Circle the verb that sounds right.

1. Don and I (drived, drove) along the new highway.
2. We (saw, seen) some new traffic signs along the way.
3. These new signs (doesn't, didn't) have any words on them.
4. They (was, were) easy to understand.
5. Don and I (thinked, thought) that these signs were helpful.
6. They (maked, made) a lot of sense to Don and me.
7. Don and I (knowed, knew) some people who could not read.

Pronouns Review

Circle the pronoun that sounds right.

8. (Me and Elroy, Elroy and I) can have the car tonight.
9. (I, Me) will ask Toni to go out with (we, us).
10. (We, Us) will go to the new movie.
11. Toni will go with (me and Elroy, Elroy and me).
12. (We, Us) will meet Tim and Elena at the movie.
13. (They, Them) live very close to the movie.
14. (Me and Toni, Toni and I) have to drive along the new highway.

★ Speaking Carefully

Read the sentences above aloud. Use the right verbs and pronouns.

Choose three verbs. Make up your own sentences.
Choose three pronouns. Make up your own sentences.
Read all your sentences to the class.

Name ______________________________ Date ______________

Writing Signs

1. What should the signs in the picture say? Write the words.
2. Make a sign to put on your desk at school.

Word Puzzles

1. Find these words in the puzzle.

detour	merge
traffic	accident
yield	danger
exit	enter

T R A F F I C
E E C A L R S
N X C H A R T
T N I O R Y O
E D D T T I D
R M E R G E A
T R N T R L N
X E T E O D G
T R A F F U E
O D A N E G R

2. Make your own puzzle. Hide the words below in it. Trade puzzles with a friend. Work each other's puzzles.

stop reduce speed drive curve

Name ____________________ Date __________

Chapter 5: READING LABELS

Word Study

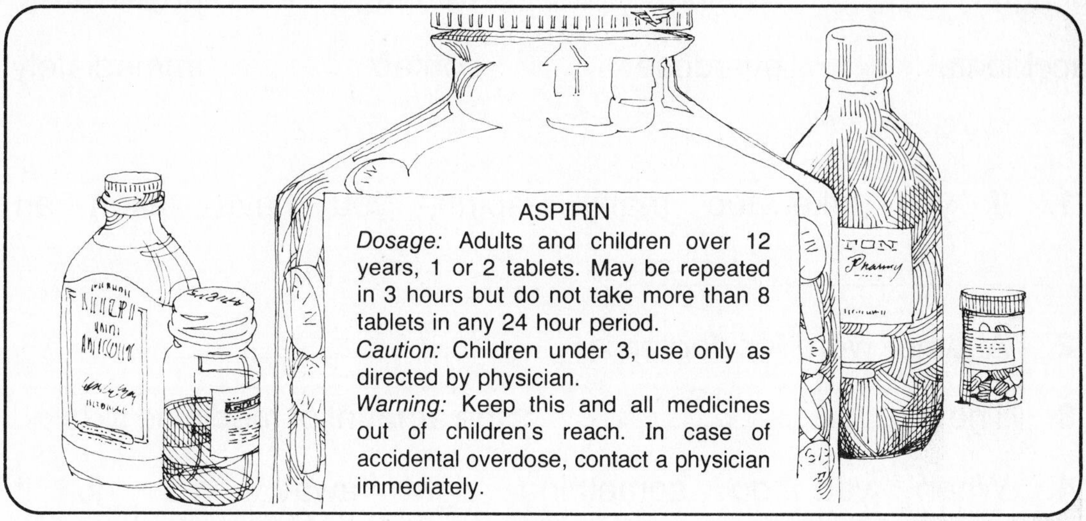
ASPIRIN
Dosage: Adults and children over 12 years, 1 or 2 tablets. May be repeated in 3 hours but do not take more than 8 tablets in any 24 hour period.
Caution: Children under 3, use only as directed by physician.
Warning: Keep this and all medicines out of children's reach. In case of accidental overdose, contact a physician immediately.

The words below are on the label shown above. Find each word in the dictionary. Write a definition for each word.

1. dosage ____________________

2. caution ____________________

3. warning ____________________

4. physician ____________________

5. accidental ____________________

6. overdose ____________________

Word Study

Use these words to complete the sentences below.

dosage	caution	warning	physician
accidental	overdose	contact	immediately

1. If you take too many aspirin, you have taken an ______________________.

2. Another word for *doctor* is ______________________.

3. The ______________________ is the amount of medicine to take.

4. When you do something right away, you do it ______________________.

5. Words that tell you to be careful are ______________________ and ______________________.

Writing Sentences

Write telling sentences. Use the words below.

6. accidental ____

____

7. dosage ____

____

8. physician ____

____

9. contact ____

____

Name ______________________________ Date ______________

Pronouns

Complete the sentences below. Read each sentence softly to yourself. Then write the pronoun that sounds right.

1. Last week ____ got the flu. (I, me)
2. ____ gave it to my brother. (I, Me)
3. __________ told our parents. (We, Us)
4. __________ called the doctor. (They, Them)
5. __________ prescribed medicine. (She, Her)
6. She prescribed one kind of medicine for __________. (I, Me)
7. She prescribed another kind for __________. (he, him)
8. Some medicine is bad for __________. (he, him)
9. __________ has high blood pressure. (He, Him)
10. ______________________________ got better. (My brother and I, Me and my brother)
11. __________ had not taken all our pills. (We, Us)
12. Our parents threw __________ away. (they, them)
13. Why did __________ do that? (they, them)
14. __________ kept them away from our little sister, Jane. (They, Them)
15. __________ cannot read labels. (She, Her)
16. She might swallow __________. (they, them)

★ Speaking Carefully

Read your sentences aloud. Listen to the sentences other students read. Did you use the right pronouns?

Writing Paragraphs

1. Write a paragraph. Tell what happened in the story above.

2. Write a sentence. Tell something important you learned from the story.

Name ______________________________ Date ______________

Medical Information Cards

MEDICAL INFORMATION CARD

Brown,	George	17
Last Name	First Name	Age

42 East Market Street
Address

Evins,	Wyoming	22001	(314) 555-2620
City	State	ZIP Code	Telephone

In case of emergency, contact:

Arden Brown	Brother
Name	Relationship

Same as above
Address

City State ZIP Code Telephone

SERIOUS MEDICAL CONDITION: Diabetes

Sometimes people carry cards like the one above.

Pretend you have high blood pressure. Complete the card below.

MEDICAL INFORMATION CARD

Last Name First Name Age

Address

City State ZIP Code Telephone

In case of emergency, contact:

Name Relationship

Address

City State ZIP Code Telephone

SERIOUS MEDICAL CONDITION: ______________________

Recognizing Sentences

Read each group of words below. Decide whether each group makes a sentence. If it does, write *yes.* If it does not, write *no.* Here are two examples:

people can read labels *yes*

labels people read can *no*

1. Very medicine is strong most. ________
2. A doctor tells you the best kind to take. ________
3. Tells you the best kind to take. ________
4. Your doctor you dosage will give the. ________
5. Your will give you the dosage. ________
6. Tells you how much medicine to take. ________
7. The dosage tells you how much medicine to take. ________
8. Medicine will not always work fast. ________
9. Will not always work fast. ________
10. You must friend not your give medicine your to. ________
11. Must not friend's medicine. ________
12. You must not take your friend's medicine. ________

Writing Sentences

Write two sentences. Write two good rules about taking medicines.

13. ____________________

____

14. ____________________

____

Name ______________________________ Date ____________

Verbs

Complete each sentence below. Pick the correct verb.

1. Yesterday my little sister ______________ home. (come, came)
2. She ______________ all the aspirin in the medicine cabinet. (ate, eaten)
3. There weren't many aspirin, but they ______________ make her sick. (did, done)
4. My sister ______________ something like that once before. (did, done)
5. She ______________ to my grandmother's house. (went, gone)
6. She ______________ out a bottle of cold tablets. (took, taken)
7. The tablets ______________ a pretty pink color. (was, were)
8. They ______________ on one of the highest shelves. (wasn't, weren't)
9. She ______________ all of them. (ate, eaten)
10. Then she ______________ to sleep. (went, gone)
11. She ______________ asleep for a very long time. (was, were)
12. I was upset at what my sister had ______________. (did, done)

★ Speaking Carefully

Read each sentence aloud. Be sure to use the right verb. Listen to sentences that others read. Were the verbs used correctly?

Word Study

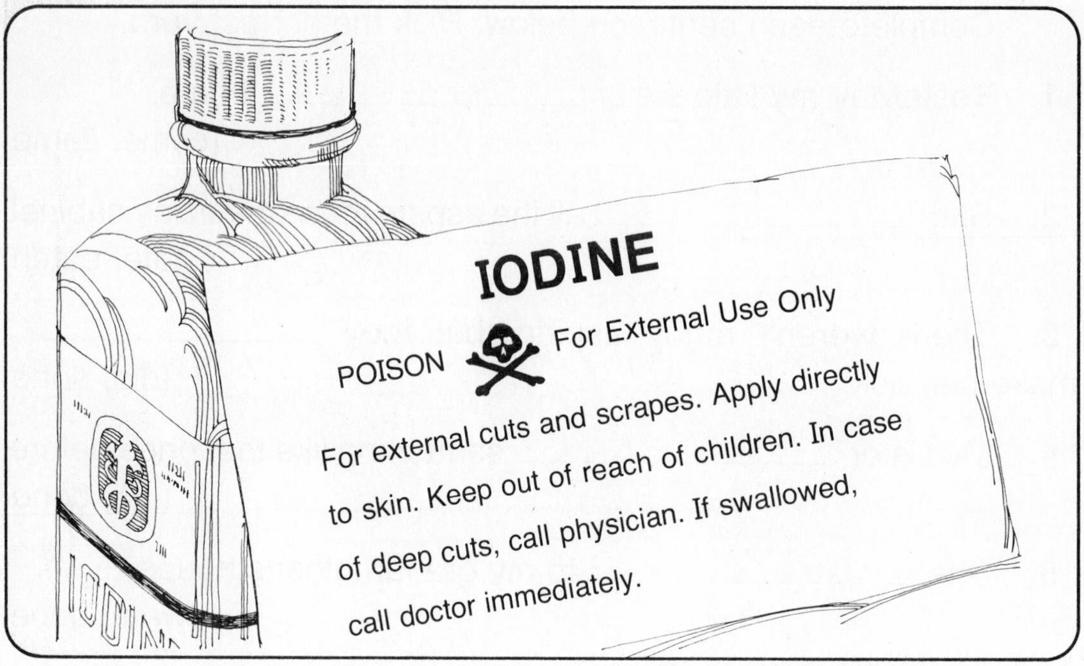

IODINE
POISON
For External Use Only
For external cuts and scrapes. Apply directly to skin. Keep out of reach of children. In case of deep cuts, call physician. If swallowed, call doctor immediately.
IODINE

The words below are on the label above. Find each word in the dictionary. Write a definition for each word.

1. poison ______
2. external ______
3. swallow ______

Writing Sentences

Use each word in a sentence.

4. poison ______

______

5. external ______

______

6. swallow ______

______

Name ______________________________ Date ______________

Discussion

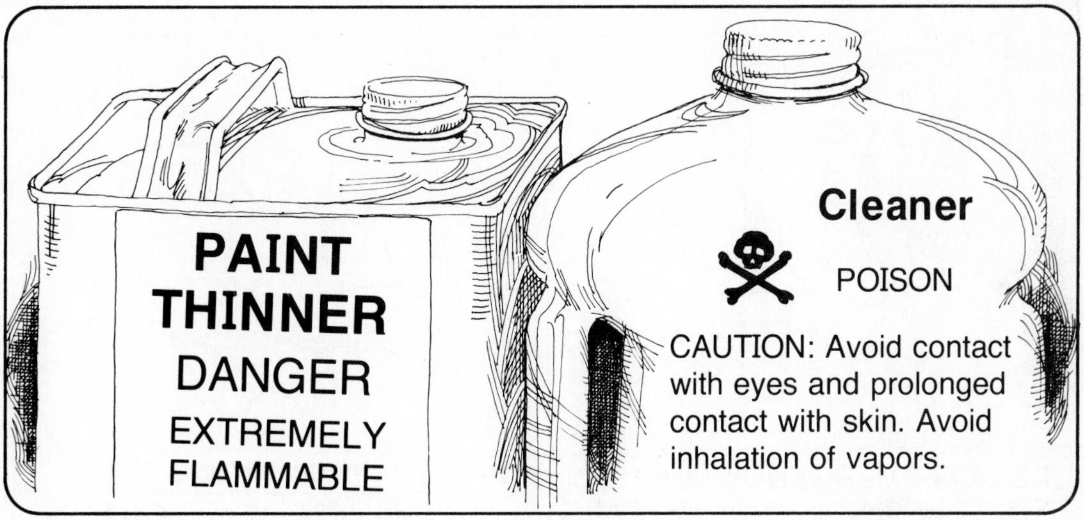

Look at the labels. Is the thinner dangerous? Is the cleaner a poison?

If people have poisons in their homes, where should they put them?

Do you have poisons at home? Do you know what they are? Are they in a safe place?

Reading Labels

Read the labels. Then answer the exercises below. If you need help, use the dictionary.

1. What does "extremely flammable" mean?

____

2. What does "avoid contact with eyes" mean?

____

3. What does "prolonged contact with skin" mean?

____

4. What does "avoid inhalation of vapors" mean?

____

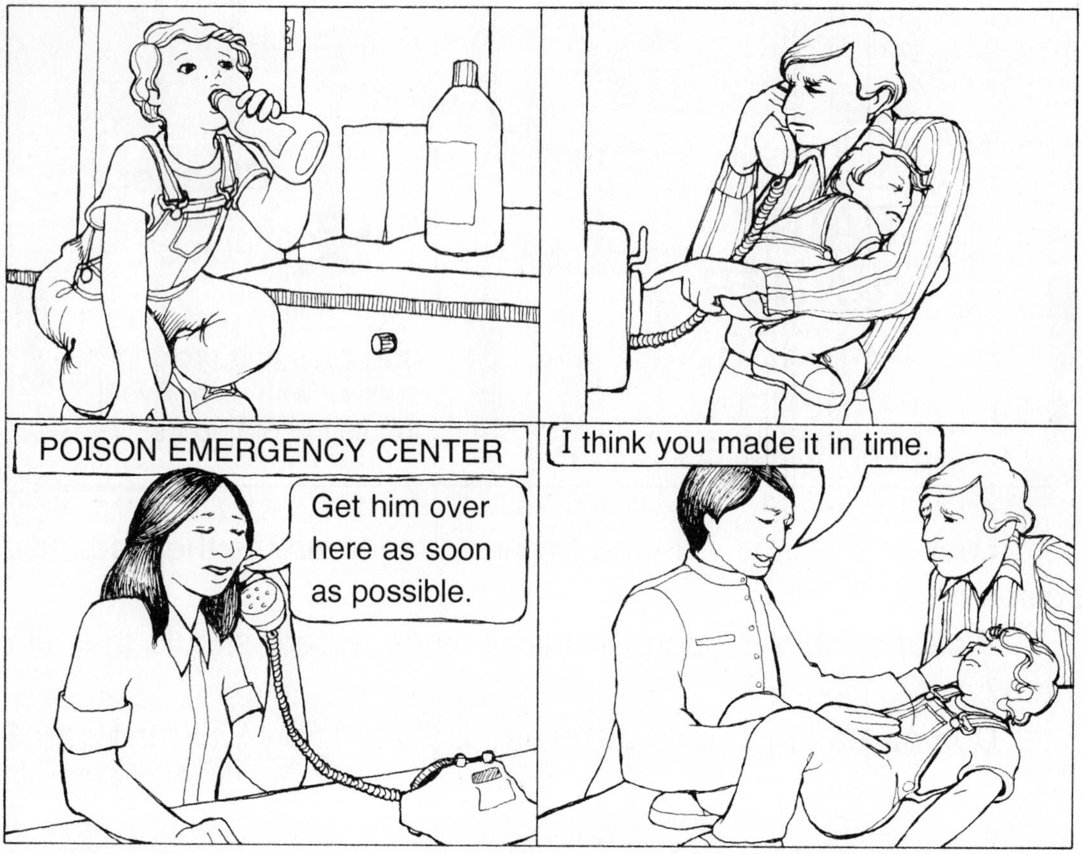
POISON EMERGENCY CENTER
Get him over here as soon as possible.
I think you made it in time.

1. Write a paragraph. Tell what happened in the story above.

2. Write a sentence. Tell why this accident happened.

Name ________________________________ Date ______________

The Telephone Directory

Yellow Pages	White Pages
PHYSICIANS AND SURGEONS	**LAMAR—CITY OF**
Aker Will 911 S. Elm----------- **727-5612**	FIRE DEPARTMENT
Alex Morris 5508 Elm --------- **532-9834**	For Emergency Calls Only----- 383-2811
Almon Mary 613 Oak---------- **831-4293**	Other Fire Calls------------------ 237-8211
HOSPITALS	POLICE DEPARTMENT
Binns Hospital 631 Grove---- **346-2913**	Emergency Number ------------ 343-2212
Cleves Hospital 381 Taylor-- **249-3643**	General Information ------------ 269-3486

If someone swallows poison, you must get help fast. You should know the telephone numbers of people who can help you.

1. Write the name and number of a hospital.

____

2. Find a doctor's name. Write the name and number.

____

3. Some fire departments can help you when someone is hurt. Write the Lamar Fire Department number to call. ______________

4. The police can help you in an emergency. Write the Lamar Police Department number to call. ______________

Writing Paragraphs

5. Write a paragraph. Tell at least three ways to get help for someone who swallowed poison.

____

____

____

____

Recognizing Sentences

Read each group of words. If a group of words is not a sentence, write *no.* If a group of words is a sentence, write *yes.*

1. What should you do if you take too much medicine? ____________
2. Should you call your doctor? ____________
3. Should you call your poison center? ____________
4. Is there in your city? ____________
5. Do you know your doctor's telephone number? ____________
6. Why your doctor's number? ____________
7. Should you take someone else's medicine? ____________
8. Why bad is it medicine to take else's someone? ____________
9. Medicine should give you friend your to a? ____________
10. Will get sick? ____________
11. Is medicine strong? ____________
12. Does medicine make you well? ____________
13. Sick can medicine make you? ____________
14. Is your friend's medicine good for you? ____________
15. Is good for your friend? ____________

You should have found seven groups of words that are not sentences. Rewrite two groups. Make sentences.

16. ____

17. ____

★ Making Signs

Make a sign. Show the name and number of a hospital.

Name ______________________ Date __________

Reading Labels

SINUS AND HEADACHE PILLS

Dosage: Adult: Two tablets, followed by one tablet every four hours. Do not exceed six tablets in 24 hours. Children (6 to 12 years): One-half adult dosage.
CAUTION: Individuals with high blood pressure, heart disease, diabetes, thyroid disease, and children under 6 years should use only as directed by physician. Drowsiness may occur.
WARNING: Keep out of reach of children.

Read the label carefully. Then answer these questions. Use your dictionary if you need help.

1. Copy the words that mean about the same as "talk to your doctor before using this medicine."

____

2. Copy the words that mean "you may get sleepy."

____

3. Ralph has high blood pressure. Should he take these pills?

____

4. Nancy is eight years old. Can she take two tablets? __________

5. Can these pills make you sleepy? __________

6. Phil is four years old. What should his parents do before they give him this medicine? __________

7. How many tablets can you take in one day? __________

★ Finding Information

Look for labels at home. Find three kinds of labels. On a separate sheet of paper, copy what the labels say.

Abbreviations

Here are some abbreviations that you might find on labels.

oz ounce or ounces

fl oz fluid ounce or fluid ounces

g gram or grams

pt pint or pints

T or tbs or tbsp tablespoon or tablespoons

t or tsp teaspoon or teaspoons

hr hour or hours

Use the abbreviations above to answer these exercises.

1. A short way to write *ounce* is ________.

2. "One T every 4 hr" means take one ________ every four ________.

3. "1 T = 3 t" means that one ________ is the same amount as three ________.

4. *Fluid* means liquid. Water and milk are fluids. Which would hold 6 fl oz: a jar of orange juice or a jar of aspirin?

____

Write the measurement words the long way.

5. 28 g ________

6. 14 fl oz ________

7. 28.35 g = 1 oz ________

8. 16 fl oz = 1 pt ________

Write these measurements the short way.

9. six fluid ounces every hour ________

10. three teaspoons ________

11. one hundred grams ________

Name ______________________________ Date ______________

Abbreviations Review

Write the new abbreviations for these states. Use the table on page 44 if you need it.

1. Arizona ________
2. Colorado ________
3. Georgia ________
4. Louisiana ________
5. Maine ________
6. North Dakota ________

Write these street addresses the short way. If you need help, look on page 38.

7. 509 West Oak Boulevard ______________________
8. 219 North Grand Avenue ______________________
9. 3124 East Larch Street ______________________

Write abbreviations for these days and months. If you need help, look on page 76.

10. Sunday ________
11. Friday ________
12. August ________
13. January ________
14. Monday ________
15. Saturday ________
16. November ________
17. February ________

Write the long form for each abbreviation below.

18. mph ______________________
19. RR ______________________
20. U.S. Post Office ______________________

★ Writing Letters

Write a short letter to someone, just to say hello. Then address the envelope. Be sure to use your return address.

Writing Sentences

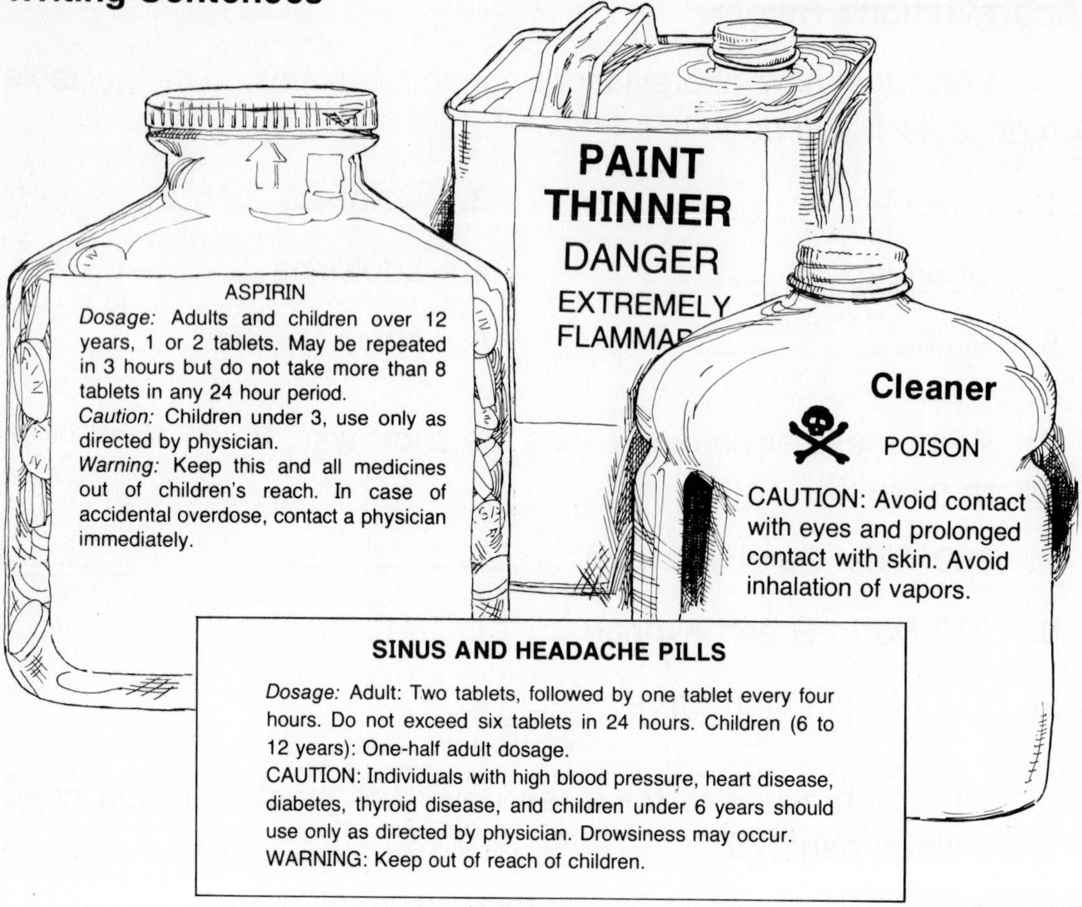

1. Write an asking sentence. Ask about the aspirin.

2. Write an asking sentence. Ask about the cleaner.

3. Write an asking sentence. Ask about the thinner.

4. Write a sentence. Answer your question about the aspirin.

5. Write a sentence. Answer your question about the cleaner.

Name ______________________________ Date ______________

Noun Plurals

Complete each sentence below. Use one of the words at the end of the sentence.

1. Many ______________________ cannot read. (child, children)

2. Their ______________________ should keep poison away from them. (parent, parents)

3. We saw ten ______________________ in the poison center. (child, children)

4. There were some ______________ with two of the children. (man, men)

5. There were some ______________________ with the others. (woman, women)

The Dictionary

To make most noun plurals, you just add an *s*.

bike bikes dog dogs egg eggs

If you make the plural a different way, the dictionary shows you how to make it.

candy (kan′ dē) *n., pl.* **candies** **sheep** (shēp) *n., pl.* **sheep**

6. In the dictionary, *pl.* means "plural." The plural of *candy* is ______________________.

7. The plural of *sheep* is ______________________.

Write the plural for these words.

8. deer ______________________ **9.** sign ______________________

10. dictionary ______________________ **11.** warranty ______________________

Reading Labels

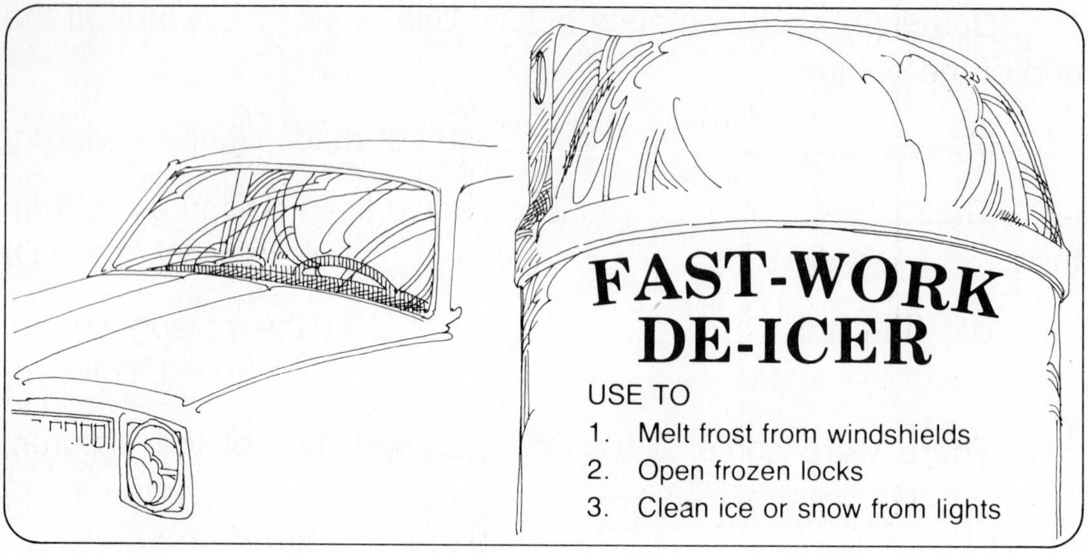

FAST-WORK
DE-ICER
USE TO
1. Melt frost from windshields
2. Open frozen locks
3. Clean ice or snow from lights

1. The label is from a can of ______________.

2. This part of the label tells you how to ______________ the de-icer.

3. How many ways can the de-icer be used? ______________

Writing Paragraphs

Grade A 100%
Unsweetened **Grapefruit Juice** 6 fl oz

4. Write a paragraph about the grapefruit juice. Tell at least three things about it.

____

____

____

____

____

Name ______________________________ Date ______________

Writing Sentences Review

doctor	medicine	children	iodine
label	cleaner	dosage	poison

The groups of words below are not complete sentences. Rewrite them. Make complete sentences. The words above can help you. Add other words where you need to.

1. important to read

____

2. can make you very sick

____

3. can help you get well

____

4. have cautions and warnings

____

5. means be careful

____

6. cannot read labels

____

7. tells how much medicine to take

____

8. is for external use only

____

9. should read the label before taking medicine

____

Understanding Sentences Review

Complete sentences make sense. Not all the groups of words below are complete sentences. Cross out the groups that are not complete sentences. Add the right punctuation mark to the end of each real sentence.

1. Cold medicines have many warnings on them___
2. Tell you not to take them___
3. Are they good for people with high blood pressure___
4. Good for people who have an eye disease called *glaucoma* ___
5. What before taking them___
6. Read the label before you take any kind of medicine___
7. Cough medicines have many warnings on them, too___
8. What should you do if your cough lasts more than a week___
9. Do you know what a *persistent* cough is___
10. Coughing often for more than a week___
11. Should examine you___
12. Should go to the doctor to see what's wrong___

Writing Paragraphs Review

Write three rules for using medicines wisely. Use complete sentences. Be sure your sentences work together.

13. ____

____

____

____

____

Name ______________________________ Date ______________

Crossword Puzzle

Fill in the crossword puzzle.

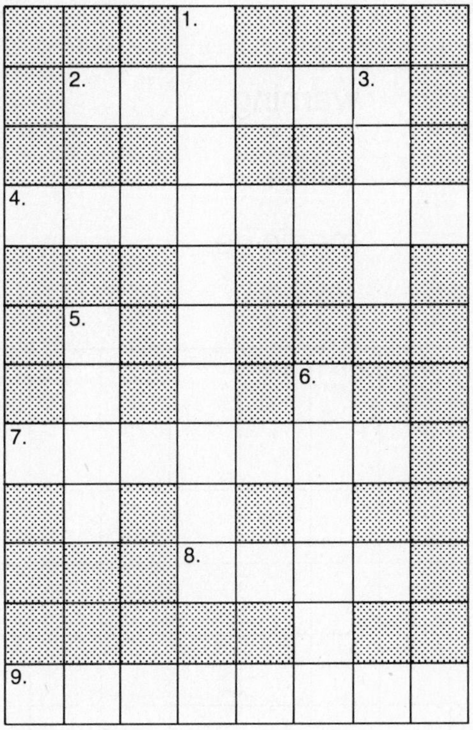

ACROSS

2. The person who tells you what medicine to take.
4. Something to take to make you well.
7. A word that means you must be careful.
8. The opposite of first.
9. Outside.

DOWN

1. A word that means you did not do it on purpose.
3. A piece of jewelry you wear on your finger.
5. What you must do with every label you see.
6. Something that can kill you.

Word Puzzles

1. Make your own puzzle. Hide the words in the puzzle below. Then give your puzzle to someone else. Ask that person to find the words.

dosage	warning	caution
doctor	nurse	aspirin
poison	medicine	external

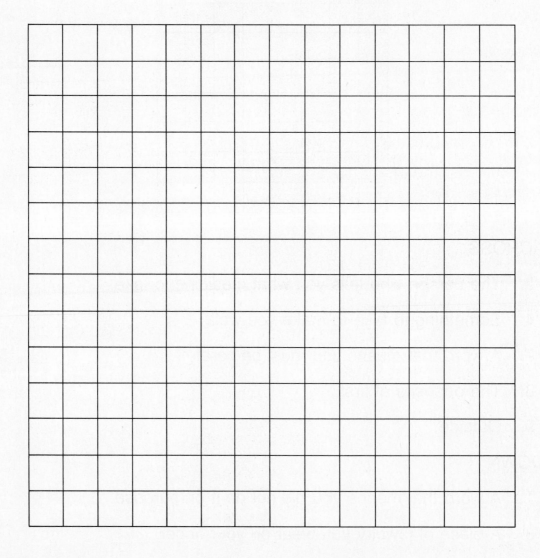

2. Add letters to make these words longer. See who can make the longest words. and keep car

Name ______________________________ Date ______________

Chapter 6: FILLING OUT FORMS

Discussion

Everybody has dreams for the future. What are yours? Would you like to buy a car? Would you like to have your own home? Do you want a job?

Will you have to make plans? Should you think about the work you will do? Do you know how to save money? Whatever you do, you will need to fill out forms.

Writing Paragraphs

Write a paragraph. Tell some of your plans for the future.

____

____

____

____

____

____

Proofreading

Do your sentences work together? Did you indent the first line?

Completing Forms

Complete the form below. Pretend you completed your driving test this morning. You got a score of 87.

APPLICATION FOR STATE DRIVER'S LICENSE

Last Name First Name Middle Initial

Address

City State ZIP Code Telephone No.

PERSONAL DATA

Height Weight Color of Eyes Color of Hair

Sex Date of Birth Place of Birth

Physical Disabilities

DRIVER'S TEST DATA

Date Passed Score Received

I hereby certify that the information on this form is complete and correct to the best of my ability.

<table>
<tr><td colspan="4">FOR OFFICE USE ONLY</td><td>M</td><td>Sa</td></tr>
<tr><td colspan="4" rowspan="2">Location Officer</td><td>T</td><td>Su</td></tr>
<tr><td>W</td><td></td></tr>
<tr><td rowspan="3">Test Form</td><td></td><td></td><td></td><td>Th</td><td></td></tr>
<tr><td></td><td></td><td></td><td>F</td><td></td></tr>
<tr><td></td><td></td><td></td><td></td><td></td></tr>
</table>

Signature

Examining Officer

Name ______________________ Date __________

The Dictionary

Find the words below in the dictionary. Write what each word means.

1. physical ______________________

____

2. disabilities ______________________

____

3. certify ______________________

____

4. ability ______________________

____

Writing Sentences

Use each word in a sentence.

5. physical ______________________

____

6. disabilities ______________________

____

7. certify ______________________

____

8. ability ______________________

____

★ Finding Information

Find three things that are poisons. Read the warnings on the labels. Copy the warnings on a separate sheet of paper.

Commas

Use commas in a list of three or more words.

Men, women, and children have to fill out forms.

Put commas where they belong in the sentences below.

1. We fill out forms when we buy houses cars or motorcycles.
2. People fill out a form when they get a license to drive hunt or fish.
3. Your relatives friends and neighbors fill out forms.
4. Forms are used by people who want jobs loans or licenses.
5. You give your name address and telephone number on forms.
6. Sometimes you give your parents' names addresses and ages.
7. Some forms ask about you your parents and your school.
8. They may ask about your education health and job experience.
9. They may ask about your age height weight and place of birth.
10. Your parents teachers or employers can help you.

★ Using the Telephone

Pretend to call the driver's license office. Introduce yourself. Say that you are learning about forms in school. Ask if you can have sample forms. You would like to practice filling them out. Tell where to mail the forms. Say "thank you" before you hang up.

Name ______________________________ Date ____________

Completing Forms

Many forms ask for the information called for below. Fill out the forms.

			Date
Last Name		First Name	Middle Initial
Address			
City	State	ZIP Code	Telephone Number
Place of Birth: City		State	Country
Date of Birth: Month		Day	Year

Date			
Last Name		First Name	Middle Initial
Address			
City	State	ZIP Code	Telephone Number
Place of Birth — City		State	Country
Date of Birth — Month		Day	Year

Commas

Add commas where they belong in the sentences below.

1. To fill out some forms you must know the day month and year when you were born.

2. Some forms will ask for your father's first last and middle names.

3. You may have to give your mother's first last and middle names.

4. Some forms ask for your height weight and eye color.

5. You need to know your name address telephone number and Social Security number.

6. Every man woman and student over sixteen years of age should have a Social Security card.

7. The Social Security form asks for your first last and middle names.

8. It asks for your mother's first last and maiden name.

9. It asks for your father's first last and middle name.

10. It asks for the day month and year when you were born.

11. It asks for the city state and county where you were born.

★ Writing Letters

Write a letter to Acme Tool Company, 123 First Street, Adrian, Ohio 63429. Ask them to send you an employment application.

★ Explanations

Read exercises 1–11 again. Then tell the class what the exercises say. You may need to make notes.

Name ______________________ Date ____________

The Social Security Form

ID CN DO

APPLICATION FOR A SOCIAL SECURITY NUMBER 742

DO NOT WRITE IN THE ABOVE SPACE

See Instructions on Back. Print in Black or Dark Blue Ink or Use Typewriter.

1 Print FULL NAME YOU WILL USE IN WORK OR BUSINESS (First Name) (Middle Name or initial – if none, draw line ___) (Last Name)

2 Print FULL NAME GIVEN YOU AT BIRTH

6 YOUR DATE OF BIRTH (Month) (Day) (Year)

3 PLACE OF BIRTH (City) (County if known) (State)

7 YOUR PRESENT AGE (Age on last birthday)

4 MOTHER'S FULL NAME AT HER BIRTH (Her maiden name)

8 YOUR SEX MALE ☐ FEMALE ☐

5 FATHER'S FULL NAME (Regardless of whether living or dead)

9 YOUR COLOR OR RACE WHITE ☐ NEGRO ☐ OTHER ☐

10 HAVE YOU EVER BEFORE APPLIED FOR OR HAD A SOCIAL SECURITY, RAILROAD, OR TAX ACCOUNT NUMBER? NO ☐ DON'T KNOW ☐ YES ☐ (If "YES" Print STATE in which you applied and DATE you applied and SOCIAL SECURITY NUMBER if known)

11 YOUR MAILING ADDRESS (Number and Street, Apt. No., P.O. Box, or Rural Route) (City) (State) (Zip Code)

12 TODAY'S DATE

14 NOTICE: Whoever, with intent to falsify his or someone else's true identity, willfully furnishes or causes to be furnished false information in applying for a social security number, is subject to a fine or not more than $1,000 or imprisonment for up to 1 year, or both.

13 TELEPHONE NUMBER

Sign YOUR NAME HERE (Do Not Print)

TREASURY DEPARTMENT Internal Revenue Service FORM SS-5 (2-73) ☐RESCREEN ☐ASSIGN ☐DUP ISSUED Return completed application to nearest SOCIAL SECURITY ADMINISTRATION OFFICE

Reading Carefully

Complete the form. Then answer each question below.

1. What names do you have to give for your mother?

____

2. What names do you have to give for your father?

____

3. What do you have to tell about the place where you were born?

____

4. What names do you have to give for yourself?

____

5. What do you have to tell about the date of your birth?

____

Organizing Paragraphs

When you write a paragraph that tells how to do something, write what comes first. Then write what comes second. Next, write what comes third. At the end, write what comes last.

Here are four things to do to get a Social Security card.

Fill out the form.

Take the completed form back.

Go to the post office or Social Security office.

Get an application form.

1. Write the four things to do. Use the correct order.

First, ______________________________

____

Second, ______________________________

Third, ______________________________

Last, ______________________________

Here are some things to do to get your driver's license.

Take tests.

Get a learner's permit.

Practice driving and learn driving rules.

2. Write the things to do. Use the correct order.

First, ______________________________

Next, ______________________________

____

Then, ______________________________

Name ______________________ Date __________

Organizing Paragraphs

Sometimes we must fill out an emergency form. This form gives a name to call if we get sick or hurt. Here are four things to do about the emergency form.

Write the information on your emergency form.

Think about who would be a good person to call.

Find out that person's address and telephone number.

Ask that person whether he or she would be good to call.

1. Write the four things to do. Use the correct order.

First, ______________________

____

Second, ______________________

____

Third, ______________________

____

Last, ______________________

2. Write a paragraph. Tell three of the first things you do in school each day. Use the right order.

____

____

____

____

____

3. Write a paragraph. Tell four things you do when you get up in the morning. Use a separate sheet of paper.

Writing Paragraphs

1. Write a paragraph about the picture. Tell what you think happened.

____

____

____

____

____

Emergency Form

2. Who should be notified in case of an emergency? Complete the form below. Write the name, address, telephone number, and relationship of that person to you.

In case of emergency, notify:

____
Full Name

____
Address

____
Telephone

____
Relationship

Name ______________________________ Date ____________

Using Pronouns

Rewrite each sentence below. Replace the underlined words with pronouns. Replace the word *Reader* with the pronoun *I* or *me.*

1. Don asked Mary to go along.

____

2. Don and Reader have gone there before.

____

3. Reader asked Lucy to go with Reader.

____

4. Our friends have visited Don and Reader.

____

5. Jeannette invited Jack to the play.

____

6. Jeannette and Jack are good friends of Don and Mary's.

____

Writing Sentences

Use each pronoun in a sentence.

7. he ______________________________
8. she ______________________________
9. me ______________________________
10. us ______________________________

★ Speaking Carefully

Make sure you used each pronoun correctly. Then read all the sentences aloud.

Abbreviations

We use many abbreviations to fill out forms. Sometimes we use numbers to show dates.

11/21/64

November 21, 1964

Read these dates. Write them the long way.

1. 1/31/72 ____________________
2. 12/2/21 ____________________
3. 3/4/26 ____________________
4. 4/4/44 ____________________

Write these dates the short way.

5. September 16, 1937 ____________________
6. May 20, 1942 ____________________
7. March 4, 1924 ____________________
8. January 17, 1925 ____________________

Write the abbreviations. For help, see pages 38, 44, 75, or 76.

9. feet ____________
10. Sunday ____________
11. August ____________
12. inches ____________
13. California ____________
14. New Jersey ____________
15. boulevard ____________
16. Pine Avenue ____________

★ Writing Letters

Write to Careers School, 130 Jones Street, Lee, Utah 24932. Ask for information on the courses it offers. Ask how much courses cost. For help, look on page 49.

Name ______________________________ Date ____________

Employment Forms

Many employment forms ask for an *employment history.* Some forms want the history in last-to-first order. Here is part of Lyndon Johnson's employment history:

1963–1969: President of the United States

1961–1963: Vice-President of the United States

1949–1961: United States Senator

Here is Eleanor's employment history:

1911–1912: Waitress, Sweet's Soda Fountain

1917–1919: Secretary, Sweet's Company

1913–1916: File clerk, Sweet's Company main office

1. Write Eleanor's employment history. Put her jobs in last-to-first order.

____

____

____

Many forms ask for your *educational history.* Here is Jack's educational history:

1943–1946: Cormo High School

1940–1943: Belcher Junior High School

1935–1940: Anderson Grade School

2. Write Jack's educational history. Use last-to-first order.

____

____

____

Employment Applications

Fill out the forms below. If you do not have an employment history, write *none*.

EMPLOYMENT HISTORY

Employer Name and Address	Position and Supervisor	Dates Worked
Last or Present		
Previous		
Previous		

EDUCATIONAL HISTORY

Dates	School and Address

★ Finding Information

Look at help-wanted ads in the newspaper. Find ads that ask for part-time help. Cut out four ads that tell about jobs you think you could do. Write why you could do one of the jobs.

Name ______________________ Date __________

Paragraphs

Here are some things to do when you apply for a position.

Find the name and address of a company that wants help.

Go to that company's employment office.

Ask for an application form.

Fill out the form.

Give back the completed form.

1. Write the things to do. Use first-to-last order.

First, ______________________

____

Next, ______________________

Then, ______________________

After that, ______________________

Last, ______________________

2. Write a paragraph. Tell four things you will do after you get home from school. Use first-to-last order.

____

____

____

____

____

____

____

____

Personal References

Mr. Forrester, I think you may do a good job. Before we hire you, though, we will need to check your references.

Employment forms often ask for references. The people who may hire you will want to talk to people who know you. They may ask whether you are honest and whether you can do the job.

Think of three people who could be personal references for you. Write their names. Then write the other information.

1. ______________________________

Last Name First Name Middle Initial

____

Address

____

Position Relationship

2. ______________________________

Last Name First Name Middle Initial

____

Address

____

Position Relationship

3. ______________________________

Last Name First Name Middle Initial

____

Address

____

Position Relationship

Name ______________________________ Date ____________

Using Verbs

Complete each sentence. Choose the correct verb.

1. Yesterday ______________ a good day for Gene. (wasn't, weren't)
2. He ______________ that he was late. (saw, seen)
3. He ______________ his breakfast too fast. (ate, eaten)
4. He ______________ out to the car. (run, ran)
5. He ______________ too fast. (drived, drove)
6. He never ______________ the police officer. (saw, seen)
7. Now he ______________ even later. (was, were)
8. When he got to the office, he ______________ up the steps. (run, ran)
9. He said that he had ______________ to get a job. (come, came)
10. Someone ______________ him a form to fill out. (gave, given)
11. He ______________ sure what the form said. (wasn't, weren't)
12. He ______________ afraid to ask for help. (was, were)
13. He just ______________ away. (went, gone)
14. Do you think he ______________ the right thing? (did, done)
15. What do you think he should have ______________? (did, done)

★ Speaking Carefully

Read your sentences aloud.

Completing Forms

Forms often look different. Many of the questions are the same. Look at these forms. You know the answers to all these questions. Read the forms carefully. Put the answers where they belong.

1. ____

Mother's Name (first, last, maiden)

____

Father's Name (first, last, middle)

____

In Case of Emergency, Notify

2.

Date	Social Security Number	
Name		
Street Address		
City	State	ZIP
Telephone		
Place of Birth		
Date of Birth		
Height	Weight	Sex

3. Telephone No. ☐☐☐ ☐☐☐☐☐☐☐
A.C.

Soc. Sec. No. ☐☐☐ ☐☐ ☐☐☐☐

Date

☐☐	☐☐	☐☐☐☐
Mo.	Day	Year

Name ______________________________ Date ______________

Completing Forms Review

Complete these forms.

1.

EDUCATIONAL HISTORY

Dates	School and Address

2. Circle highest grade completed in school:

Grade School	High School	College
1 2 3 4 5 6 7 8	9 10 11 12	13 14 15 16

3.

EMPLOYMENT HISTORY

Employer Name and Address	Position and Supervisor	Dates Worked
Last or Present		
Previous		
Previous		

Punctuation Review

Some of the sentences below need commas. Add commas where they belong. Add the correct end punctuation.

1. Sometimes it is hard to decide whom to call in case of a fire accident or other emergency___
2. The person should be responsible available and willing___
3. After filling out a form, you sign your name___
4. Will you sign your name right away___
5. Do you understand everything on the form___
6. You may need to ask a parent relative lawyer or friend if you should sign___
7. Can you get in trouble if you sign something you don't understand___
8. Wow, you surely can___
9. Don't sign leases loans or other documents if you don't understand them___

★ Punctuation Puzzle

If you read the lines below as a poem, they do not make sense. If you can find the sentences, the lines do make sense. Try to make the lines make sense. Add punctuation and capital letters to show the sentences.

I walk to school on a bike you see

a sign that it's for sale for free

you'll get a smile from a honey bee

you just get honey do you agree

Name ______________________________ Date ______________

Crossword Puzzle

Work this crossword puzzle. Use some of the words that you see below.

maiden	bike	cold	last
address	night	day	hot
middle	first		

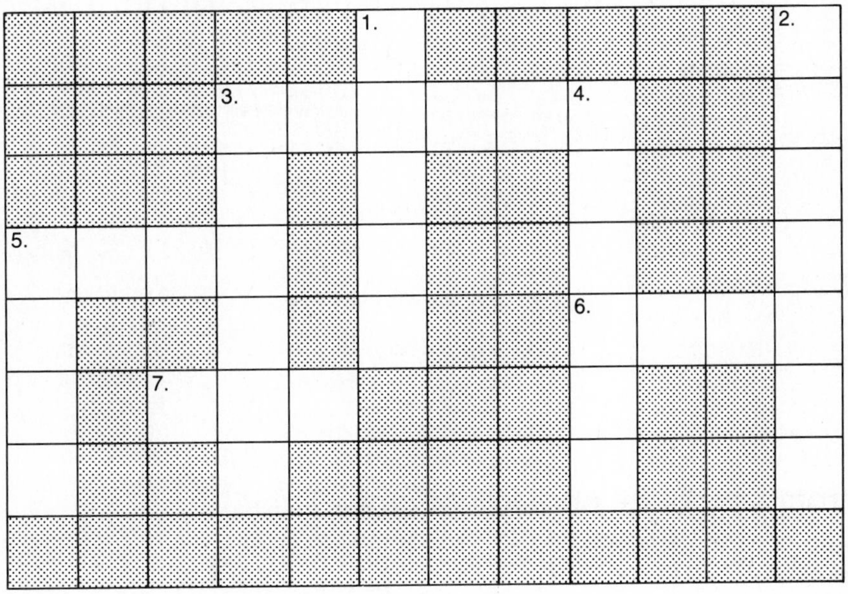

ACROSS

3. One kind of name you have to know for your mother.
5. What the Social Security office will give you. It has a number on it.
6. Something that has two wheels.
7. Something that is not new.

DOWN

1. When the moon comes up.
2. The number and street where you live.
3. One kind of name you have to know for yourself.
4. What your Social Security card has on it.
5. Something that is not hot.

Puzzles

1. Find these words in the puzzle:

security	number	middle	initial
social	emergency	address	important
notify	maiden		

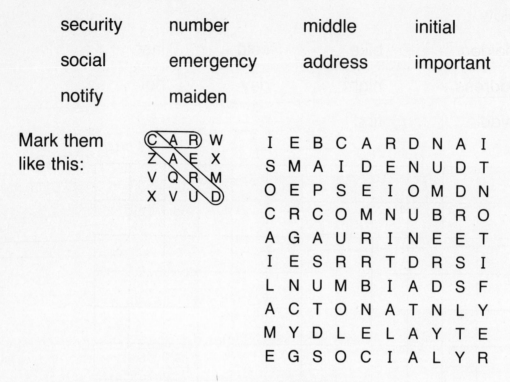

Mark them like this:

C	A	R	W
Z	A	E	X
V	Q	R	M
X	V	U	D

I	E	B	C	A	R	D	N	A	I
S	M	A	I	D	E	N	U	D	T
O	E	P	S	E	I	O	M	D	N
C	R	C	O	M	N	U	B	R	O
A	G	A	U	R	I	N	E	E	T
I	E	S	R	R	T	D	R	S	I
L	N	U	M	B	I	A	D	S	F
A	C	T	O	N	A	T	N	L	Y
M	Y	D	L	E	L	A	Y	T	E
E	G	S	O	C	I	A	L	Y	R

2. Go from school to job. Do not cross lines.

Name ______________________________ Date ______________

Chapter 7: FINDING A JOB

Reading Carefully

Answer each question below.

1. What kind of job did Leon have before? ______________
2. What does Maysie's Restaurant need? ______________
3. What will Ms. Jones do for Leon? ______________

____

4. What will Leon do next? ______________

____

★ Explaining

Do you know what a bus boy does? Explain what you do at that job. If you don't know, explain another job.

Interviews

Leon will go to Maysie's Restaurant. He will talk to Mrs. Maysie Burns. Answer these questions about the interview.

1. Will Mrs. Burns ask Leon about his work experience? ______
2. Will she want to know his Social Security number? ______
3. Will she ask for references? ______
4. What are references? ______

______

5. Will she want to know where he went to school? ______
6. How should Leon dress? ______
7. Should Leon be on time for the interview? ______
8. How should Leon talk? ______
9. Is it all right for Leon to ask questions? ______

Write three questions that Leon might ask.

10. ______

______

11. ______

______

12. ______

______

★ Answering Questions

Pretend you are being interviewed. Answer these questions: Do you have any work experience? Can you give three references? Do you have any questions about the company?

Name ________________________________ Date ______________

Employment Application

Complete the employment application below.

APPLICATION FOR EMPLOYMENT

Date ______________________

Name ____
(Last) (First) (Middle)

Address ____
(Number) (Street) (City) (State)

Telephone ________________ Social Security ________________

Married ________________ Single ________________

EDUCATION

SCHOOL	DATES ATTENDED		GRADUATED/DEGREE
College ________	______	______	________
High School ________	______	______	________
Elementary ________	______	______	________

EXPERIENCE

NAME OF EMPLOYER	ADDRESS	TYPE OF WORK	DATES
________	________	________	____
________	________	________	____
________	________	________	____
________	________	________	____

LIST ANY SPECIAL SKILLS (TYPING, ETC.)

____

REFERENCES

Name ________________ Name ________________

Address ________________ Address ________________

________________ ________________

Signature ________________________________

Reading Classified Ads

Ads often have abbreviations. Here are some abbreviations.

Abbreviation	*Word*	*Meaning*
appt.	appointment	time to meet
drv. lic.	driver's license	driver's license needed
eve.	evening or night	you work nights
exper., exp.	experience	work you have done
hswk.	housework	
lt.	light	
nec.	necessary	you must have it

Rewrite each ad. Change the abbreviations to words.

RELIABLE PERSON, lt. hswk., exper. nec. 990-3567 after 5:00.

1. ____

____

PERSON to drive older person to doctor. Drv. lic. nec. No exper. needed. 567-7654 before 3:00.

2. ____

____

____

LT. HSWK., eve. and Sat. No exp. nec. Call for appt. 222-0091.

3. ____

____

____

Name ______________________________ Date ______________

Reading Classified Ads

Here are more abbreviations from the classified ads.

Abbreviation	*Word*	*Abbreviation*	*Word*
hrly.	hourly	per mo.	each month
bldg.	building	per wk.	each week
bus.	business	ref. req.	references required
co.	company	sal.	salary
per hr.	each hour	start	to start out with

Rewrite each ad. Change the abbreviations to words.

SALES. Ref. and exp. req. Sal. $560 per mo. Call for appt. Arthur Farker, Allen Co., 345-5555.

1. ______________________________

____

____

BOOKKEEPING. Exper. nec. Start sal. $175 per wk. Box 34A, 65440.

2. ______________________________

____

____

LT. HSWK. Drv. lic. nec. Ref. req. Sal. $125 per wk. Call Martin Hay 333-0097.

3. ______________________________

____

____

Capitalization and Punctuation

Here is an interview between Jenny Allen and Mr. Wilshire. Put a circle around each word that should start with a capital letter. Put the correct mark at the end of each sentence. Some groups of words are more than one sentence.

J: good afternoon, mr. wilshire i am jennifer allen everyone calls me jenny

Mr. W: hello, jenny i am happy to meet you please sit down

J: thank you, mr. wilshire i am happy to meet you, too

Mr. W: jenny, i have read your application it looks very good i see that you have never worked for an electric company before do you mind if i ask you a few questions

J: no, mr. wilshire, i don't mind at all

Mr. W: jenny, why do you want to work at emmons electric

J: i have heard that it is a good company i will graduate from high school in two months i will want a good, steady job i am sure i can learn to do the job that you have open

Mr. W: i like your answer, jenny i think you will be a good worker you can start part-time next week you can work full-time after you graduate now i will introduce you to mrs. wicking she will be your boss welcome to emmons electric, jenny

J: thank you very much, mr. wilshire

★ Interview Practice

Work with a friend. Let one person be Jenny. Let the other person be Mr. Wilshire. Act out the interview.

Name ______________________________ Date ______________

Writing Sentences

Write a sentence to answer each question below. The questions are the kinds of things that an interviewer might ask you.

1. Good morning. How are you today?

____

2. Won't you sit down?

____

3. Did you have any trouble finding my office?

____

4. Do you mind if I take a few minutes to read your application?

____

5. I see that you're still in school. When will you graduate?

____

6. Have you ever worked in a place like this before?

____

7. Do you think you can learn how to do this job?

____

8. Why do you want to work here?

____

9. I think we will give you a chance. When can you start to work?

____

★ Practicing Interviews

Let a friend ask the interview questions. Read your answers. Then change roles.

Your Clothes and Speech

Clothes that you wear for fun may not be right for a job interview. On an interview, dress carefully. Be clean and neat. Comb your hair. Wear nice clothes.

You should speak correctly, too. With your friends, you don't always think about the way you talk. On a job interview, be polite. Don't use slang.

Some of the sentences below are for friends only. Some can be used on a job interview. Write *F* after sentences that are for friends only. Write *J* after sentences that can be used on a job interview.

1. Good morning. I am glad to see you. ____
2. Hi ya. How you doin'? ____
3. Thank you for taking the time to see me. ____
4. Yes, I worked there for three years. ____
5. Yeah, I had this job a couple years. So what? ____
6. Huh? Come again? Watcha say? ____
7. Pardon me, I didn't hear you. ____

★ Speaking Carefully

Read your *J* sentences aloud. Speak clearly and pleasantly.

Name ______________________________ Date ____________

Writing Sentences

The sentences below may work in talk among friends. They are not good for a job interview. Rewrite each sentence. Change the "street talk" to "work talk."

1. Hi, how ya doin'? ______________________________

2. I ain't seen you for a long time. ______________________________

3. I been gone outta town. ______________________________

4. I seen my sister. ______________________________

5. How come you ain't told nobody? ______________________________

6. You ain't gone yet, has you? ______________________________

7. Did you ate them hot dogs? ______________________________

8. They was for lunch. ______________________________

9. Now we ain't got nothin' to eat. ______________________________

★ Speaking Carefully

Read your sentences aloud. Speak clearly. Speak pleasantly.

Finding Sentences

Read this job interview. Some of the word groups are more than one sentence. Find the sentences. Circle each word that should start with a capital letter. Add the correct end punctuation marks.

HARRY: good morning, mrs. evans thank you for letting me talk with you about the job you have open

MRS. E: come in and sit down, harry give me a few minutes to read your application i haven't seen it yet do you mind waiting

HARRY: i don't mind take your time i'll be happy to answer any questions you have

MRS. E: well, harry, you did a good job on this application i have just one question

HARRY: yes, mrs. evans, what is your question

MRS. E: when can you start

HARRY: you mean i have the job thank you, mrs. evans you won't be sorry i can start on monday

MRS. E: i'm sure i won't be sorry, harry i'm glad you'll be working with us i'll see you on monday morning then

HARRY: it has been a pleasure to talk with you, mrs. evans

★ Interview Practice

Ask a friend to work with you. Take parts in the interview. Read the parts to each other.

Work with a friend. Write an interview. Then read your interview to the class.

Name ______________________________ Date ______________

Word Study

Here are some words you should know:

personnel	employee	interview
application	employer	appointment
references	experience	salary

Use these words to complete the exercises below. If you need help, use your dictionary.

1. An office that deals with people is a ______________ office.

2. The amount of money you make is your ______________.

3. A worker is an ______________.

4. When you ask for a job, you may be asked to fill out an ______________ form.

5. When you have a set time to meet someone, you have an ______________.

6. People who will put in a good word for you are your ______________.

7. An ______________ hires workers.

8. When you have worked before, you have ______________.

9. When you talk to someone about a job, you have an ______________.

★ Finding Information

Look in newspapers or magazines. Find pictures of clothes. Cut out five outfits that can be worn on job interviews. Paste them on a sheet of paper.

Writing Business Letters

SALES CLERK, no exp. nec. Send qualifications to Mae Bright, Quality Stores, 18 Main, Akron, OH 73272

DRIVER, familiar with city. State driving experience. Write P.O. Box 312, Essex, NH 02932

Write a letter. Answer one of the ads above. Use page 49 if you need help.

Name ________________________________ Date ______________

Job Interviews

The picture above shows two job interviews.

1. Tell what you think happened in interview *A.* Tell why.

____

____

____

2. Tell what you think happened in interview *B.* Tell why.

____

____

____

3. Why should you be polite and friendly on an interview for a job?

____

____

★ Making Up Interviews

Work with a friend. Make up interviews to match each picture.

Writing Business Letters

JUNE GRAD. Opening in Sales Dept. for beginner with good typing skills. Write Box AE, Daily News, Avon, ME 20601

ORDER DEPT. CLERK. We train. Apply by letter only. Jones Engineering, 1831 N. Main, Derek, AZ 31201

Write a letter to apply for one of the jobs above.

Name ______________________________ Date ______________

Puzzles

1. Find these words in the puzzle. *Warning:* Some of the words are spelled backwards in the puzzle.

employer	employment	confident
application	application	polite
interview	interviewer	correct
appointment		
friendly		
questions		
transportation		

R	E	W	E	I	V	R	E	T	N	I	Q	Y	T
U	Q	T	N	E	M	Y	O	L	P	M	E	U	I
C	O	N	F	I	D	E	N	T	F	O	R	F	N
N	O	I	T	A	T	R	O	P	S	N	A	R	T
Q	C	R	Q	S	P	O	L	T	I	E	R	I	E
R	U	A	R	U	E	P	O	L	I	T	E	E	R
A	R	P	U	E	M	P	L	O	Y	E	R	N	V
A	P	P	L	I	C	A	T	I	O	N	E	D	I
A	P	L	I	C	A	T	I	O	C	A	N	L	E
T	N	E	M	T	N	I	O	P	P	A	D	Y	W
E	O	S	N	O	I	T	S	E	U	Q	N	D	I
S	C	T	E	R	R	O	C	C	O	R	E	T	C

2. Draw the kinds of clothes to wear on a job interview. If you can't draw, look in a newspaper or magazine. Find the right kinds of clothes. Paste them here.

Understanding Taxes

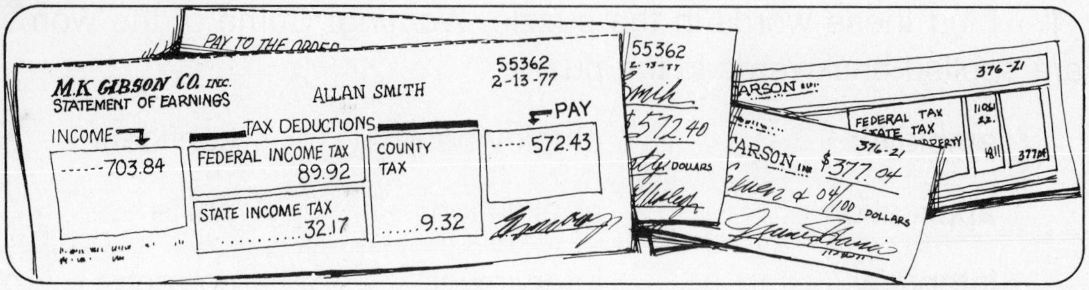

When you make money, you pay taxes. These taxes help pay for schools, streets, and other things. You may pay taxes to your city, county, state, and country.

You may have to pay income tax. You may have to pay a personal property tax. There are forms to fill out for these taxes.

The income tax forms ask how much money you make. The personal property tax forms ask how many things you own.

Discuss these questions. Then write your answers.

1. Do people pay a federal income tax where you live? ________
2. Do people pay a state income tax? ________
3. Do people pay a city or county income tax? ________
4. Do people pay taxes on real estate? ________
5. Do people pay taxes on personal property? ________
6. Do people pay a sales tax? ________
7. Name three things that taxes pay for in a city or county.

____

8. Name three things that taxes pay for in a state.

____

9. Name three things that taxes pay for in our nation.

____

Name ______________________________ Date ______________

Reading Tax Instructions

The government has booklets on how to fill out your income tax form. Part of one Index to Instructions is shown above.

1. Is the index in alphabetical order? __________

Tell the page on which you would find these things.

2. How to *figure* your tax. ____

3. What *address* to use when you mail in your form. ____

4. Whether you must *file* a form. ____

5. The rules for a *single person.* ____

6. What *records* you must keep. ____

7. Information about *refunds.* ____

8. Whether to use Form 1040. ____

Income Tax Form

Complete the income tax form. Pretend that your wages were $8,768.34. You had no other income. Your adjustments were $2,516.00 Your tax was $1,176.00.

INCOME TAX FORM Individual Tax Return 19____

Please Print or Type		
	Your Full Mailing Address	Your Social Security Number
		Your occupation
	Your Present Employer and Address	

Filing Status		Exemptions	
	1a ☐ Single		2a ☐ Yourself
	1b ☐ Married filing joint return		2b ☐ Spouse
	1c ☐ Married filing separately		3a ☐ Children
	1d ☐ Unmarried Head of Household		
	1e ☐ Widow(er) with dependent		4 ☐ Total Exemptions

Taxes		
5 Wages, Salaries, Tips	5	
6 Other income	6	
7 Total (Add lines 5 and 6)	7	
8 Adjustments to income	8	
9 Adjusted income (Subtract 8 from line 7)		
10 Tax from Tax Table		

Sign here		
	▶ Your signature — Date	▶ Signature of Preparer other than taxpayer — Date
	Spouse's signature (if joint return) — Date	Address

Name ______________________ Date __________

Loan Applications

Sometimes people borrow money. To borrow money, you fill out a loan application. Complete the application below. Use your own name and address. Use today's date.

You work as a kitchen aide at Arden's Beanery, Arden, Idaho. You have been there two years. Your salary is $6,700. Your boss is Ellen Arden. You have a savings account, #10-401. It has $300. You have a checking account, #24-098-099, with $75. Both accounts are at the Seven Seasons Bank. You have no other assets or credit cards.

CREDIT APPLICATION — Through the First Friendly Bank
TOM'S CYCLES — Seven Seasons, Idaho

Please Print

Last Name ______ First Name ______ Initial ______ Date ______

Address ______ Soc. Sec. No. ______

City ______ State ______ ZIP ______ Phone ______

EMPLOYER

INCOME SOURCES

Name ______ Address ______

Your position ______ Salary per yr. ______

Length of time employed ______ Supervisor ______

OTHER ASSETS

Savings: Number ______ Bank ______ Amount ______

Checking: Number ______ Bank ______ Amount ______

CREDIT REFERENCES

Your Bank ______ Address ______

Credit Card ______ Expiration ______

Credit Card ______ Expiration ______

Signature ______ Date ______

Puzzles

1. Go from home to the bus stop to the employment office by the shortest possible way. *Do not cross any lines!*

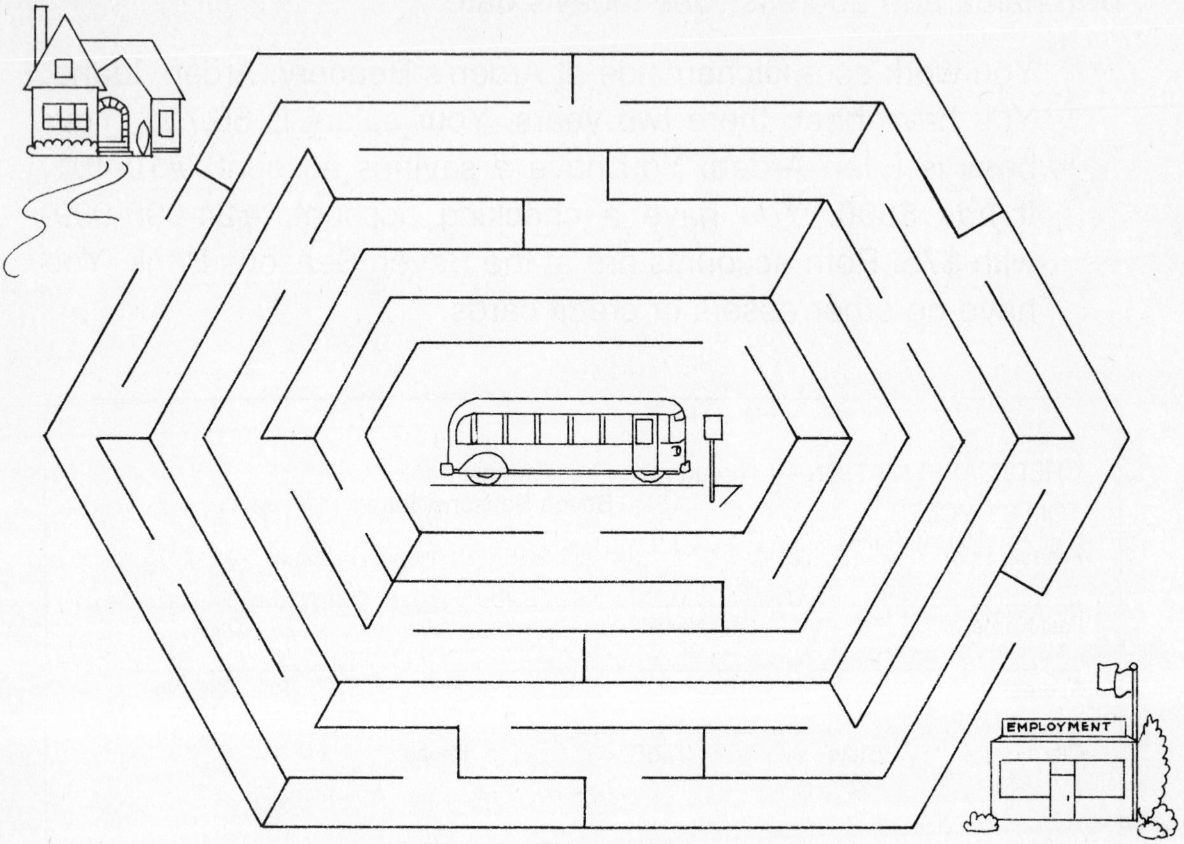

2. Unscramble the letters below. Make words you had in this chapter. Write the words on the lines.

mlopynemet ____________ toppliacain ____________

nertiwive ____________ obj ____________

3. Make six words by rearranging letters in this word:

transportation

____________ ____________

____________ ____________

____________ ____________

Name ______________________________ Date ______________

Chapter 8: TRAVEL AND RECREATION

Discussion

Do you know what recreation is? Recreation is what we do for fun. What do you like to do for fun? Can you think of hobbies that people like? Can you think of games that are fun? What sports are good recreation? Some people travel as part of their recreation. Where would you like to go for fun? Are there zoos or museums or other interesting places near you?

Do you think that everyone needs recreation? Why is recreation important to us?

1. Name a hobby that you could have. ______________________
2. Name a game that you could play. ______________________
3. Name a zoo or museum near you. ______________________
4. Name a sport that you could enjoy. ______________________
5. Write a paragraph. Tell what people can do for recreation.

____

____

____

____

Sports

There are many sports that we can enjoy. Read the list of sports below. Think about whether you might like each one. For each sport write *yes* or *no.*

1. Bicycling ____________ **2.** Bowling ____________

3. Jogging ____________ **4.** Swimming ____________

5. Calisthenics ____________ **6.** Badminton ____________

7. Walking ____________ **8.** Skiing ____________

9. Skating ____________ **10.** Volleyball ____________

11. Softball ____________ **12.** Soccer ____________

13. Tennis ____________ **14.** Hockey ____________

15. Horseshoes ____________ **16.** Archery ____________

17. Golf ____________ **18.** Basketball ____________

Answer these questions about the sports.

19. Which do you think costs the most money? ____________

20. Which do you think costs the least money? ____________

21. Which is easiest to do? ____________

22. Which is hardest to do? ____________

23. Name two sports you like. ____________

____

24. Name a sport you don't like. ____________

★ Explaining

Think about some of the sports you like. Explain to your classmates why you like them.

Name ________________________________ Date ______________

Planning Your Time

Read the story. Then answer each question below.

1. When must Denise and Bill leave Denise's house? __________
2. When does Denise want to leave her house? __________
3. When will Bill be finished with his job? __________
4. When would Bill like to get to Denise's? __________
5. Can Bill go to the game? __________
6. Explain why you answered exercise 5 as you did.

____

____

____

____

Using Verbs

Complete each sentence below. Use a different verb in each sentence. Use more than one word if you wish.

1. Don ____________________ movies.

2. He ____________________ them every time he can.

3. Movies ____________________ money.

4. That's why Don ____________________ the money he makes at his job.

5. Don ____________________ the bus when he goes to movies.

6. He ____________________ when the buses go past his house.

7. He ____________________ the schedule.

8. Don ____________________ to movies early in the evening.

9. The bus ____________________ him to the movies on time.

Use each word in a sentence. Use the word as a verb.

10. like (*or* likes) ____________________________________

____

11. read (*or* reads) ____________________________________

____

12. find (*or* finds) ____________________________________

____

13. watch (*or* watches) ____________________________________

____

14. stop (*or* stops) ____________________________________

____

Name ______________________________ Date ______________

Plural Nouns

Nouns that name more than one person, place, or thing are called **plural nouns.** We make some plural nouns by adding an *s:*

bike bikes pool pools

We make some plural nouns by adding *es:*

box boxes mess messes

We make some plural nouns by changing the word:

man men foot feet

Write the plural form of each noun below. If you are not sure about a word, look it up in the dictionary.

1. woman ______________	**2.** ticket ______________
3. dress ______________	**4.** movie ______________
5. arrow ______________	**6.** baseball ______________
7. car ______________	**8.** player ______________
9. theater ______________	**10.** skate ______________
11. child ______________	**12.** stitch ______________

Write asking sentences. Use the plural nouns in your asking sentences.

13. gardens ______________________________

____

14. tents ______________________________

____

15. geese ______________________________

____

16. games ______________________________

____

Commas in Series

Put commas where they belong in the sentences below.

1. Harry Martina Alfredo Dolly and Mary know how to get around in their city.

2. They know how to use buses taxicabs and subways.

3. Does your city have buses taxicabs and subways?

4. Can buses subways and taxicabs be found in every city town and village in the United States?

5. Harry Martina Dolly Mary and Alfredo use buses to get to restaurants parks and bowling alleys.

6. Sometimes Harry Martina Alfredo Dolly and Mary ask their friends to go to the show with them.

7. Their good friends are Eddie Mark Ann and Tina.

8. When Eddie and Tina drive, Harry Martina Alfredo Dolly Mary Mark and Ann don't take the bus.

9. Buses taxis and subways are good when you don't have a car.

10. Does using buses taxis and subways save gas?

Using Pronouns

Rewrite exercises 5 and 6. Make each sentence shorter by using pronouns instead of nouns.

11. ____

____

12. ____

____

Name ______________________________ Date ______________

Reading Schedules

BUS SCHEDULE, LIMIT/STADIUM EXPRESS
Average time between Limit Avenue and Stadium Corners is 53 minutes.

Leaves Limit Avenue
A.M.: 5:15, 5:45, 6:15, 6:45, 7:15, 7:45, 8:15, 8:45

Leaves Stadium Corners
A.M.: 6:15, 6:45, 7:15, 7:45, 8:15, 8:45

BASEBALL SCHEDULE

Home Games: Razorton Rockets
*Night game: 8:25 P.M.
**Day game: 12:00 noon

May 11 Edgerton Tigers*

May 17-20 Staunton Stingers*

May 21 Velker Vikings**

June 1 Aurora Owls**

MOVIE SCHEDULE

Stardew
Fried Fish 5:15, 6:45, 8:15, 9:45

Timber
Lady in Distress 1:45, 4:20, 7:00, 9:30

Union Ave. Flicks
The Fatal Hand 8:15

Viewtone
Dominoes and Diamonds 1:15, 3:15, 5:15, 7:15, 9:15, 11:15

1. How long does it take to ride from Limit Avenue to Stadium Corners on the bus? ______________________

2. You want to see the Rockets play the Tigers. When must you get to the stadium? ________________

3. You are going to a movie at 1:15. Which movie will you see?

____

4. At which time can you see *The Fatal Hand*? ______________

5. You want to see the first showing of *Lady in Distress.* You need a half hour to get there. When should you leave home?

____

Writing Sentences

Write a complete sentence to answer each question.

1. What movie theaters are showing *Sportacular?*

____

2. When is *Sportacular* showing?

____

3. What movie theaters are showing *Keep 'Em in Stitches?*

____

4. When is *Keep 'Em in Stitches* showing?

____

★ Finding Information

Find the movie section in your newspaper. On a separate sheet of paper, write the name of a movie you would like to see. List the place or places where this movie is showing. Write all the times that the movie is shown.

Name ______________________ Date __________

Reading Maps

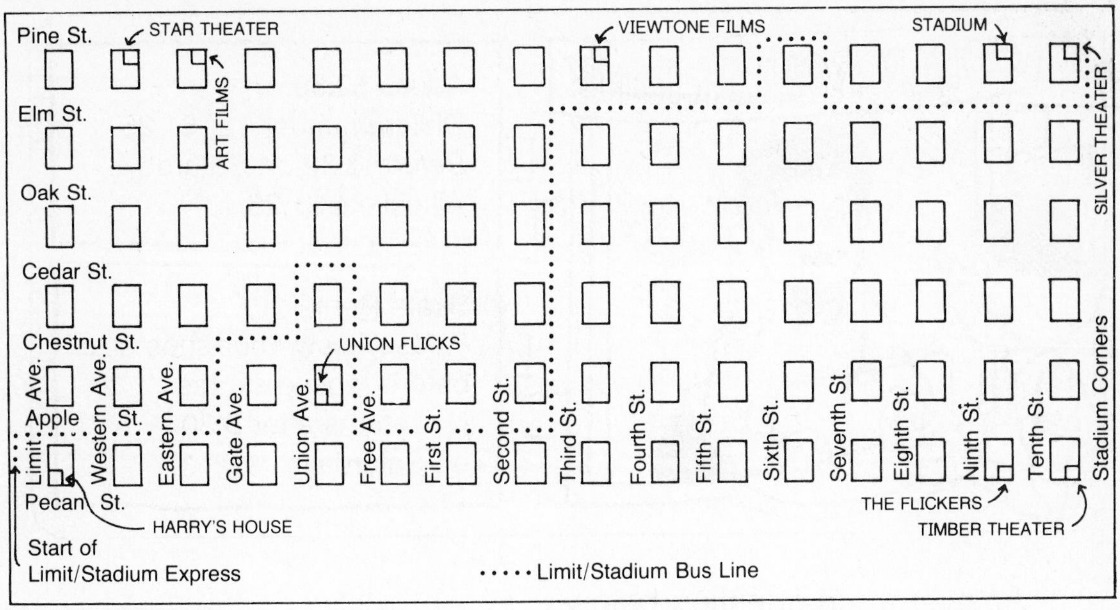

Look at the map. Answer each question below.

1. Which theaters are on the route of the Limit/Stadium Express? ______________________

2. Which theaters are not near the route of the Limit/Stadium Express? ______________________

3. Name three streets or avenues over which the Limit/Stadium Express drives. ______________________

4. Agnes lives at the corner of Oak Street and Limit Avenue. She works at the Silver Theater. How could she get to work?

____

Planning Recreation

Answer each question below.

1. What kind of rink is the World Rink? ______________________

____

2. It is Saturday. Nell is sixteen years old. How much will she pay for a ticket? ______________________

3. How much will she pay on Monday? ______________________

4. What is for rent? ______________________

5. Why do people need to know their shoe sizes? ______________________

____

6. What is your shoe size? ______________________

7. Does your town have a roller skating rink? ______________________

8. Does your town have an ice skating rink? ______________________

9. Are the rinks listed in the telephone book? ______________________

10. How could you find out when a rink is open? ______________________

____

Name ______________________ Date ____________

Planning Money

1. How much money is this man's paycheck worth? ____________

2. He gets this much money every week. About how much will he get in a month? ____________

3. How much is his rent bill? ____________

4. Do most rent bills come once a month? ____________

5. About how much salary will be left after he pays his rent? ____________

6. Does he have other bills to pay, too? ____________

7. Will he also have to buy food? ____________

8. About how much will food cost him for one month? ____________

9. Do you think he is paying too much rent? ____________

10. What should he do? ____________

____

★ Discussion

What things do people spend money for? How much money do you think a single person spends on these things? If you made $450.00 per month, about how much rent could you pay?

Newspaper Ads

You can use the classified ads in the newspaper to find places to live. Classified ads have many abbreviations. Here are some abbreviations.

Abbreviation	*Meaning*	*Abbreviation*	*Meaning*
attr.	attractive	apt.	apartment
sm.	small	trans.	near transportation
per mo.	each month	bdrm.	bedroom
ref. req.	references required	bal.	balcony
furn.	furnished (has furniture)	mgr.	manager

Read the classified ads below. Rewrite each ad. Write complete words instead of abbreviations.

1. NEW: Attr. apt., 2 bdrms., bal., mgr. lives on premises. Rent: $350.00 per mo. Two-year lease req. Ref. req. Call Archer Apts., 333-3333.

____

____

____

____

2. GREAT VALUE: Sm. apt., 1 bdrm., trans. See mgr. 3476 Bellevue. $135.00 per mo. Ref. req. Furn.

____

____

____

Name ______________________________ Date ______________

Airline Travel

Circle all the words that should start with capital letters. Add the correct end punctuation mark.

1. this lesson tells about getting airline tickets___
2. where would you like to go on an airplane___
3. do you know how to get your ticket___
4. will you use the telephone to find out about tickets___
5. pretend you want to go to akron, ohio___
6. first, look in your telephone book___
7. find the telephone numbers of airline offices___
8. next, call these offices___
9. will you ask about flights to akron, ohio___
10. ask how much a ticket to akron, ohio, will cost___
11. is coach class cheaper than first class___
12. does the airline have an excursion rate___
13. ask if a meal is served___
14. are meals free on planes___
15. ask how you can get your ticket___
16. can it be mailed to you___
17. do you get it at the airport___
18. write down the answers to your questions___

★ Explanations

Read exercises 1–18 again. Then tell the class how to get an airline ticket.

Traveling by Train

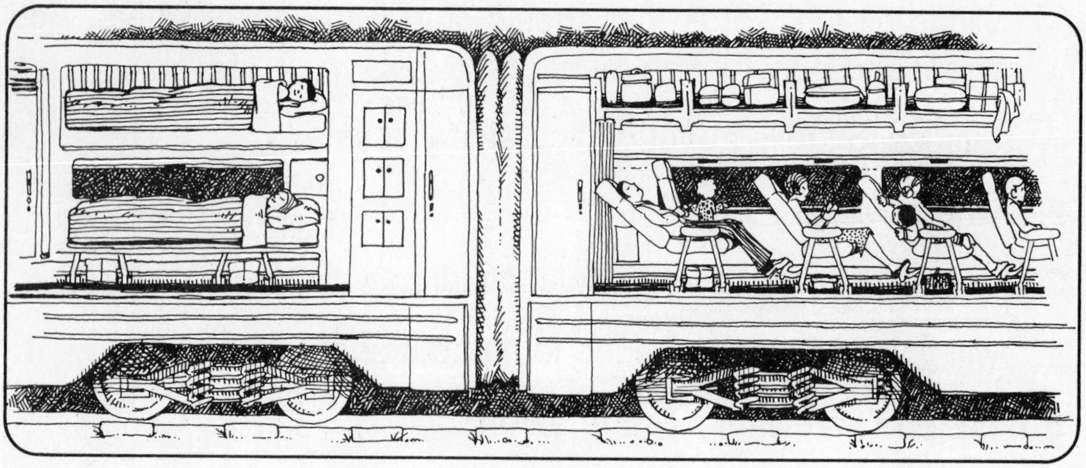

Like airplanes, trains have coach and first-class tickets. Coach tickets cost less than first-class tickets. If you get a coach ticket, you have a chair. It tilts back so you can rest on a long trip. With a first-class ticket, you have a chair during the day. You also have a bed at night. A train is slower than an airplane. You may spend many hours on a train to get where you are going. That's when a bed really feels good! Some trains serve meals. Meals on trains are not free.

Write three ways that trains are different from planes.

1. ______________________________

2. ______________________________

3. ______________________________

Write two questions to ask if you call about railroad tickets.

4. ______________________________

5. ______________________________

★ Finding Information

Check your telephone directory. Are any railroads listed there? Can you tell if those railroads carry passengers?

Name ______________________________ Date ______________

Traveling by Bus

Buses are different from planes and trains. They do not have coach and first-class tickets. All tickets on buses are the same class. Buses go many places where trains and planes do not. Almost every town has a bus station.

Planes and trains have food for the passengers to eat. Buses do not. Buses stop every few hours. Everyone gets out to eat. On a long bus trip, you get on and off the bus many times.

Write a paragraph. Name a place that you would like to visit. Tell whether you would go by bus, train, or plane. Tell why you would go that way.

____

____

____

____

____

★ Planning Trips

Plan a trip someplace. Figure out how much it would cost. Tell the class about your trip.

Reading Maps

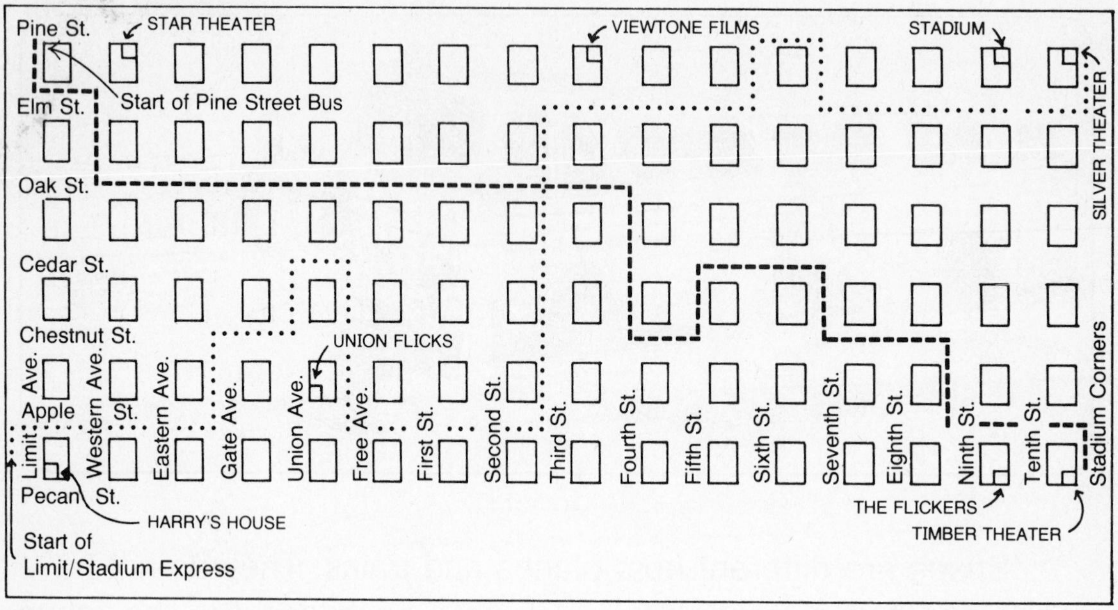

Look at the map. Answer each question below.

1. To go to the Silver, Harry takes the ____________________ ____________________.

2. To go to the Timber, he takes the ____________________ ____________________ to the corner of ____________________ and ____________________.

3. There, Harry transfers to the ____________________ ____________________.

4. To get home from the Timber, Harry takes the ____________________ ____________________ to the corner of ____________________ and ____________________.

5. At that corner, he will transfer to the ____________________ ____________________.

Name ______________________________ Date ______________

Singular and Plural Nouns

Complete each sentence below. Read each sentence quietly to yourself. Then write the words that sound correct.

1. ______________________ has a very good zoo.
(This city, These cities)

2. ______________________ have a very good zoo.
(This city, These cities)

3. ______________________ like to picnic in the park.
(A person, People)

4. ______________________ likes to picnic in the park.
(A person, People)

5. __________________________ has to reserve a place.
(A big group, The big groups)

6. __________________________ have to reserve a place.
(A big group, The big groups)

7. __________________________ pets the animals in the children's zoo.
(Amy, Amy and John)

8. __________________________ pet the animals in the children's zoo.
(Amy, Amy and John)

9. ______________________ likes to watch the monkeys.
(A child, Children)

10. ______________________ like to watch the monkeys.
(A child, Children)

11. __________________________ takes a lot of food on a picnic.
(Leon, Leon and Dina)

12. __________________________ take a lot of food on a picnic.
(Leon, Leon and Dina)

13. ______________________ don't have many trees.
(This park, Some parks)

Hobbies

Do you know what a hobby is? A hobby can be almost anything you like to do. Read the list of hobbies below. Think about whether you might like each one. For each hobby, write *yes* or *no.*

1. Collecting rocks ________ 2. Playing music ________

3. Gardening ________ 4. Drawing ________

5. Knitting ________ 6. Collecting stamps ________

7. Cooking ________ 8. Photography ________

9. Collecting coins ________ 10. Making models ________

11. Woodcarving ________ 12. Collecting records ________

Some people collect coins and stamps. Name two other things that people collect.

13. ________ 14. ________

Some people make model cars. Name two other kinds of models that people make.

15. ________ 16. ________

17. Name another good hobby.

____

Write a paragraph. Tell about a hobby you like. Tell what it is. Tell how or when or where people do it. Tell why it is a good hobby.

18. ________

____

____

____

____

Name ________________________ Date ____________

Word Study

Use the dictionary. Write a definition for each word.

1. recreation ________________________

2. hobby ________________________

3. sports ________________________

4. travel ________________________

5. schedule ________________________

Writing Sentences

Use each word in a sentence.

6. recreation ________________________

7. hobby ________________________

8. sports ________________________

9. travel ________________________

10. schedule ________________________

Commas in Series

Put commas where they belong in the sentences below.

1. We can travel by plane train and bus.
2. Which way is slow cheap and fun?
3. Would you like to travel on a bus a plane or a train?
4. Leon Tom Fred and Manolo decided to take a trip.
5. They didn't have much money or time.
6. They looked at schedules for trains buses and planes.
7. They decided to take a bus to a town that was near the mountains the forests and a very large river.
8. They packed their boots swim suits and sleeping bags.
9. They decided they would hike swim and camp out.
10. They would collect wild flowers leaves and vines.
11. Leon Fred and Manolo had gone camping before.
12. Tom told Leon Fred and Manolo that he had never been camping.
13. They told him to bring lots of clothes food and cooking equipment.
14. They would sleep out on Saturday Sunday Monday and Tuesday.
15. They were going camping for fun relaxation and education.
16. Leon did not like to camp in November December January or February.
17. His favorite months were May June July and August.
18. Tom Manolo and Fred knew why Leon felt that way.
19. Was it because of money weather or something else?
20. Do you like to go camping swimming or hiking?

Name ______________________________ Date ____________

Proper Nouns

Names of places are proper nouns. Cities and states are places. Rivers, islands, parks, and museums are places, too. Read each sentence below. Circle every word that should start with a capital letter.

1. have you ever been to mount vernon?

2. mount vernon is in virginia.

3. it was the home of george washington.

4. the alamo is in san antonio, texas.

5. the statue of liberty is on liberty island.

6. the statue of liberty is in new york, new york.

7. you might like dodge city, kansas.

8. would you like to ride a mule down grand canyon?

9. the grand canyon is near flagstaff, arizona.

10. would you like to camp out in yellowstone national park?

11. would you like to see where george washington carver was born?

12. would you like to take a steamboat down the mississippi river?

13. you could go from st. louis to new orleans on the mississippi river.

Writing Paragraphs

Write a paragraph. Name three places that you would like to visit. Tell why you would like to visit those places.

14. ____

____

____

____

Writing Friendly Letters Review

1. Write a friendly letter. Tell about something you did last week.

2. Address the envelope below. Include your return address.

Name ________________________ Date ____________

Writing Paragraphs Review

1. Write a paragraph. Tell about something you like to do. Tell what it is. Tell something else about it.

____

____

____

____

____

2. Write a paragraph. Tell what you can do for fun in a large city if you don't have much money. List at least three things that are free or cost very little.

____

____

____

____

____

____

3. Write a paragraph. Tell what kind of apartment you would like to rent. Tell at least three things about the apartment.

____

____

____

____

____

____

Writing Business Letters Review

Write to the Sunshine Tourist Bureau. It is at 123 Star Street, Vista, New Mexico 13921. Say that you will take a vacation in June. Ask the Bureau Director for information about things to do in the Vista area.

____
____
____

____
____
____
____

_____________________________:

____
____
____
____
____
____
____

____
____

Name ______________________ Date __________

Pronoun Review

Write the pronoun that sounds right.

1. ________ like to go with ________.
(I, Me) (they, them)

2. ________ always pick movies ________ like.
(They, Them) (I, me)

3. Will ________ come with ________?
(he, him) (we, us)

4. ________ has a great collection of tapes.
(She, Her)

5. ________ like to listen to music with ________.
(I, Me) (she, her)

6. ________ likes jogging.
(He, Him)

7. ________ likes to ride a bike.
(She, Her)

8. ________ like to jog with ________.
(I, Me) (he, him)

9. ________ like to ride bikes with ________.
(I, Me) (she, her)

Write sentences. Use the pronouns in your sentences.

10. I ______________________________

11. us ______________________________

12. them ______________________________

Verb Review

Use each verb or verb phrase in a sentence.

1. go ______________________________

2. going ______________________________

3. went ______________________________

4. has gone ______________________________

5. forgot ______________________________

6. forgotten ______________________________

7. am driving ______________________________

8. drove ______________________________

9. driven ______________________________

★ Speaking Carefully

Read your sentences aloud. Listen to your classmates' sentences. Did you use the verbs correctly?

Name ______________________ Date __________

Employment Application

Complete the employment application below.

APPLICATION FOR EMPLOYMENT

Date ______________

Name ____
(Last) (First) (Middle)

Address ____
(Number) (Street) (City) (State)

Telephone ______________ Social Security ______________

Married ______________ Single ______________

EDUCATION

SCHOOL		DATES ATTENDED		GRADUATED/DEGREE
College				
High School				
Elementary				

EXPERIENCE

NAME OF EMPLOYER	ADDRESS	TYPE OF WORK	DATES

LIST ANY SPECIAL SKILLS (TYPING, ETC.)

____

REFERENCES

Name ______________ Name ______________

Address ______________ Address ______________

______________ ______________

Signature ______________

Puzzles and Games

1. Hide all the words in the puzzle. They can go across, up, down, or on a slant. They can even go backwards.

information	railroad	transportation	theater
bus	station	movie	class
train	travel	coach	airplane

2. Play "Travel Out." The leader picks a way to travel: land, water, or air. If the way is land, players take turns naming ways to travel on land. The first one who can't think of a way is out.